The Germans on Trial

HEINZ LUNAU

The Germans on Trial

STORM PUBLISHERS · NEW YORK

Contents

The Cause I Am Pleading

The Cause I Am Pleading

I feel compelled to speak up in defense of millions of human beings, abject criminals so-called, of whom it is said that they have sinned against all the tenets of Western civilization; that they have directly or indirectly conspired and unleashed their armored might against a world living in peace and sailing confidently, on the waves of brotherly love, into a rosy future; that they have brutally attacked and overrun innocent neighbors and have smilingly rejoiced in the moans and groans of their helpless victims; that they eagerly embraced an abominable heathen cult of race-superiority; that they set out, back in the fateful autumn of 1939, to conquer the world goose-stepping and trampling the flowers of Western civilization under their unholy boots; that they have indulged in or condoned the atrocious revival of genocide by beastly attempts to exterminate members of another race; and of whom it is now said that they are simply getting what is coming to them.

This "getting what is coming to them" is the easy formula for keeping more active concern with the entire matter at a safe distance from our minds and consciences. It is a comfortable solution and our big chance to be relieved of any further responsibility except the trouble of meting out punishment.

The situation, however, is not as simple as that. And the meting out of punishment without trial is as dangerous today as it was yesterday. As far as the German people are concerned, there has been no trial, there is no trial, and there never will be a trial other than the multitude of current events and the happenings of a recent past in which the loss of a war has set in motion an avalanche of misery with no end in sight.

To be sure, there have been post-war trials in which the might of the victors descended upon the abject crowd of Nazi chieftains and their tools. Great pains were taken in their preparation and procedure to live up to the essential requirements of law, which demand that no man be tried under an ex post facto law, that there be no accused without the help and assistance of the personification of true liberalism—the lawyer, that there be no punishment without a fair trial.

That the imperfections of so-called international law should have forced the legal tools of the victors to proceed to some pretty astute somersaults in order to live up, in appearance, to the particular rule that no man can be tried under an ex post facto law, has been bitterly criticized by thoughtful people the world over and has been regretted by many whose knowledge and position made it possible for them to discern the danger of using Nazi methods to "legalize" the disposal, by means of "law" and the noose of Nuremberg, of the political, military, and administrative scum which had been making havoc of the fate of man for a dozen years.

But a trial there was, and a chance for the accused to speak their minds, to raise their voices in defense of their deeds or misdeeds. And then there was judgment and its execution.

Not so with the German people—with countless women, children, old folks, and the remnants of the male population of Germany. For them there was no trial, and there was no judgment. But there *is* punishment. There is punishment of staggering proportions, ranging from near complete abolition of national self-determination, to the hunger eczemas of innocent children; ranging from the brutal expulsion of millions of German nationals from

their homesteads where Germans had toiled and
tilled the soil for generations, to the army of starving garbage-diggers in the cities, reduced to the
level of wild animals; from a radical disruption of
economic life and the normal pursuit of happiness
to the revival of slavery in which able-bodied men
are rotting by the millions at the mercy of the
victors. There is punishment ranging from complete despair among German youth to the inevitable rise of an army of cynics versed in the art
of racketeering and black-marketeering and the
consequent risk of the mark they will leave on a
population supposedly being re-educated and re-
habilitated according to the standards of Western
civilization; from the evitable and inevitable consequences of foreign rule to the waste of an entire
group of well-intentioned new political and spiritual leaders who are ruining their careers in timid
attempts to better the lot of their countrymen by
"collaborating" with the deputies of the victors.
There is punishment ranging from the dismantling
of factories and industry to the standardization of
famine by means of allocating so and so many cal-
ories a day.

The wrath of man has descended upon the Germans. And man shakes off his responsibilities with
the easy theme song: They are getting only what

they deserve. And yet, is it true? Do they really deserve it?

The German people got no trial. There they are, an anonymous multitude of human beings, reduced to staggering misery, passive victims of a march of events which cannot fail to call up alarming parallels with the iniquities perpetrated all over Europe by the Hitler crowd.

What was it that made decent people the world over boil when confronted with reports of the crimes perpetrated by those abject self-appointed high priests of the Nazi cult? Was it not the barbarous, brutal practice of racial persecution culminating in gas chambers and incinerators of "human garbage?"—But in the wholesale racial persecution which is being perpetrated by the Russians, Poles, and Czechoslovakians on German nationals beyond the Iron Curtain, the misdeeds of Nazism are finding a dangerous counterpart.

What was it that made decent people the world over foam with indignation at certain practices imposed upon conquered nations by Nazi warlords? Was it not the revival of slave labor imposed upon helpless foreign nationals?—Yet it is a very open question whether the Nazis' revival of slavery is not matched or even surpassed by the conditions in which the French and the Russians have held millions of German prisoners of war over the years.

What was it that made Nazi methods of holding conquered nations under their heel so repulsive to all of us living according to the standards of Western civilization? Was it not the insidious use the Nazis made of opportunists and occasional well-intentioned patriots among the conquered, who have become known all over the world as Quislings? —Compare any number of Quislings who went through their antics under the protection of Nazi police with the army of Quislings flowering in Germany today as an inevitable consequence of the present four-power rule—and again, the insidious Nazi practice of ruling by proxy resembles the work of dilettantes.

Do all our fierce and splendid reactions against inhuman practices lose their impact when the actors change? Can we honestly square the comfortable formula of the German people simply getting what they deserve, with what is actually going on?

The little enlightenment we have been able to get on the German problem has consisted chiefly in a rather detailed program as to the most practical way of administering "justice" to the Huns, of bringing those lost sheep back into the fold of decent behavior. Public discussion centers only around the punishment to be inflicted. There is little talk of whether or why. It is simply a matter of how.

For those of us who are thoughtless enough to say that in these matters there is no need for a trial, that history itself *is* the trial, that the day Nazi Germany was beaten judgment was rendered, it would be wise to try to imagine what the situation would be like, had the Germans and their Allies won the war.

No person in his right mind in this or any other country belonging to Western civilization can believe that the historical accident of the loss of a war would turn lies about the American people into truths. Do you think, for instance, that some twenty million American voters who did not vote for Roosevelt in 1944 would not be outraged at being punished for the politics of President Roosevelt—not to mention the millions of non-voters? Do you think Americans would not make a point of the decency of their individual lives and of the little, if any, influence they had on the course of current events, were they faced with the hypothetical victors' decision that they must be punished for having made war on Germany? Do you think Americans would not rebel against the accusation that they were anti-German hate-mongers, Indian-killers, gangsters who are getting only what is coming to them? Do you believe the good people of Ohio would not find it difficult to persuade themselves that they were getting only what they deserved if they were forced to submit reforms in their children's educational program to some Japanese officer for approval in the name of the occupying power? Do you think the miners of Pennsylvania might not feel tempted to say something rather expressive about the idea that they should be held responsible for the past political leadership of their land, and do you not think they might be very eager to slow down on their jobs if they looked at their starving women and children and realized that the product of their efforts was being used to feed the industrial centers of Japan?

Fortunately this is only an hypothetical sketch of what might have happened. And I rejoice in the fact that this war was conducted and won against the evil forces of dictatorship and Nazidom preponderantly by a nation which stands for the heritage of Western civilization. I rejoice all the more in this accident of history since it allows me to take up the cause of the German people.

My plea for the Germans is addressed to the American public, an indefinite number of jurors, a jury of plain, ordinary people whom I would like to call common Americans. My plea is addressed to those whose superficial knowledge of foreign people is of necessity based on what they have been told. It is submitted to those who have accepted what they were told for no other reason than that hard-working people find it impossible to devote more than fleeting moments to gathering information on a "bunch of foreigners" who, to all appearances, are the root of all the ills which have befallen this world. My plea is addressed to those who have been unsuspecting victims of the output of the mass book-publishing trade and of a press whose more widely read organs thrive on their appeal to our primitive curiosity and interest in sensational tales, reports, and pictures. My plea is presented to a jury of Americans who got thoroughly acquainted with the more repulsive aspects of Nazi torture without being informed that the abject tools of Nazism who perpetrated these beastly acts belonged to a small category of social outcasts from all parts of Europe. My plea is addressed to a jury of Americans who were thoroughly informed of the atrocious Nazi policy of persecution of the Jews, but who heard little, if anything, about the innumerable cases where Germans, disregarding danger, punishment, and death, stuck to their Jewish friends and helped them wherever they could against the monsters of Nazism. My plea is addressed to those who heard in minute detail about the outrageous crimes of the infamous SS Special Einsatz Commandos who perpetrated their abominable henchmen's jobs behind the back of the German armies, but who have scarcely ever been informed that those Himmler brutes were chosen from among the crop of congenital sadists in all the conquered and several unconquered countries of the continent. My plea is addressed to those who were fed with tales about the Gestapo and its activity in conquered countries, being thus led to forget that the real task of the Gestapo, from the moment it was created, was to hold Germany and the *Germans* in an iron grip.

When I decided to take up the cause of the Germans, I did not forget the atrocious character of the social disease—the Nazi pest—with which the Germans suffered ever since a group of ruthless public-welfare gangsters got away with murder through trickery, deceit, and the full-scale exploitation of hitherto unknown methods of propaganda; I did not forget about the vicious acts the Nazis perpetrated on the Germans, the Jews, and the world at large; I did not forget how amazing it was to realize that such a disease could break out among a nation which had occupied a pre-eminent place within the Western world and its intricate civilization. And if I dare to submit a plea for my people, I want it to be understood that it is for the huge mass of hard-working, decent, honest Germans, who are the backbone of my country as such people are the backbone of any civilized country, that it is for the huge mass of Germans who throughout their history have tried very hard to master their lives in decency that I raise my voice.

Knowing them as I know myself, I do not have to rely on the superficial pieces of information which the glamor boys and girls of the newspaper trade see fit to throw at the public; I do not have to draw on an ever-growing pile of volumes on the Germans and the German question written by God knows whom, for God knows what purpose; I do not have to rely on predigested opinions taken from history books, from Tacitus to Emil Ludwig; I do not have to adjust my arguments to any purpose linked with political ambition, to the exigencies of any public office, to simple vanity or hatred or whatever the special motives may be which prod individuals of various backgrounds and often dubious qualifications to advocate a certain stand on this or that problem of public concern.

My plea will have none of the impassioned, emotion-sweeping character people think of when a lawyer sets out to address a jury. The case exceeds by far the possibilities of the most artful piece of forensic niceties. It is not my aim to accuse or to excuse; what I will try to do is to explain, in human terms, in terms of our civilized existence, what happened to the Germans. I hope to be able to give *the* explanation—the one which could relieve the rest of the world of the expensive and unpleasant illusion of having some seventy million barbarians and schizophrenic criminals around who have to be kept in chains.

I shall aim to give an explanation which will reaffirm our confidence in the values of Western civilization, an explanation which will make it easier for millions of decent people to live along carrying their cross of being Germans, an explanation which may make it possible for the world to go on *with* the Germans taking a positive part in humanity's efforts toward better and greater spiritual and material accomplishments. I shall try to give an explanation designed to convince the jury of the necessity of modifying conditions under which the Germans (as any other people in similar conditions), out of sheer desperation, might again fall victim to another political magician or even sell their souls and skills to the East.

I shall try to explain that it is not innate wickedness but the very attributes of civilized human beings which made it possible for a part of the German population to be tricked into casting their lot with the Nazis; that what happened to the Germans might have happened to any people—given a similar set of external circumstances; that there is nothing wrong with the Germans that a little good will and understanding on the part of the victors cannot set right. I shall try to explain how vital it is to correct the widespread error of attempting to elucidate national, political, and social questions by looking at individuals and their individual make-up, instead of looking at such questions as what they really are: social problems.

They Had It Coming, Didn't They?

1. The Prosecutor's Bias

You will have heard a number of opinions about the German people, nearly all of them selected and presented with the zeal which is the attribute of any public prosecutor, in this case a number of self-appointed manufacturers of flaming indictments or subtle insinuations, designed to convince you, the jury, that the Germans are getting only what they deserve, and maybe not enough of it.

If all these opinions detrimental to the Germans were true, that is, if they corresponded to what really was and is, the defense would indeed be pleading a lost cause. But I mean to prove that the bulk of the prosecution's accusations are untrue.

I mean to make clear to you that Nazism is not the apotheotic expression of Prussianism; that the Germans are not possessed of innate wickedness and vice which opinion-mongers interpret as brute barbarism, wholesale paranoia or schizophrenia; that the German people are not a "Robber Barons, Inc." driven by an irresistible thirst for domination; that they are not a race whose laziness makes them wait for the propitious moment to unleash their viciousness on the peace-loving nations of the earth; that the ever-recurring French refrain of "three wars made by Germany in the last seventy-five years" belongs to that same realm of fancy and is far from constituting conclusive proof of the Germans being the curse of this earth.

If those opinions were true, not only would I be fighting a lost cause, not only should I be failing the ethics of the lawyer's profession, but the Germans would be getting what is coming to them—and indeed "not enough of it."

The acceptance of such opinions is responsible for the prevailing lack of interest in the whole series of current events known as world-history-in-the-making and which, for years to come, will shape the very existence of generations of human beings.

Newspapers and periodicals in this country voiced amazement when the first reports reached here that the American boys in the European theater of war seemed to prefer the Germans to any other people with whom they had come into contact. To persons convinced of the basic wickedness of the Germans, such reports do not make sense. And the only logical conclusion is that the "opinions" which were injected into unsuspecting minds by war-bred propaganda or special interests simply do not tally with the facts.

In the same vein I might mention the surprise recorded in the press each time one of the polls conducted in Germany reveals that those wicked creatures, in their large majority, are by no means floored by an overwhelming sentiment of guilt, nor felled by an overpowering bad conscience. What does this mean? It means that a German, looking back at the avalanche of atrocities and evil brought upon the world by the Nazi regime, may feel like a fool for having allowed a gang of politicians to trick him into voting them into power; he may feel incredibly naïve for having joyfully accepted the end of joblessness and misery in the wake of the Nazi New Deal; he may even feel silly for having allowed his sentiments to get the better of him when he was induced to back a Nazi foreign policy said to bring justice to his people— but he cannot tolerate being treated like a criminal, for he is not aware of having committed a crime any more than you and most of the rest of us are. And if in his quiet hours he does feel haunted by a sense of responsibility and guilt, it is because what he has learned about Nazi atrocities has given him a glimpse of the beastly potentialities in the deepest abyss of the human soul; and if he is of a religious bent of mind, he will not be able to rid himself of the notion that since we were all created potentially equal, no human being—neither he nor you and I—can be exempt before God and Eternity from sharing in the responsibility and guilt of others. But if he feels that way, it is not because he happens to be a German; it is because he is a Christian or simply a human being.

Whether you of the jury have already a set of definite opinions on the Germans, whether you are seriously desirous of being able to form your own opinions or to check the opinions you have cannot be known to me. What I do know is that it is almost impossible for the general run of people to acquire the facts that are indispensable in forming an unbiased opinion. Plain living is so complicated that it takes up almost every minute of our time: job, family life, hobbies, sex, food, sleep, social relations, education—a steady flow of events and sensations and their interrelations—fill our lives from the cradle to the grave. Our vocations and avocations are too absorbing for most of us to wish or even to be materially able to devote more than fleeting moments to questions which, at first glance, appear to have no immediate connection with our individual lives. Books make it by no means easier to know what is actually going on; on the contrary, they add to our confusion. And when it becomes too difficult to cut through the web of words in which the riddle of man's life in society appears to be enveloped, we easily and sometimes even eagerly escape into "opinions."

We acquire such "opinions" in various accidental ways conditioned by our education, the contacts we make, the surroundings we live in. Too often we feel no urge to submit them to the test of our own experience and intelligence. We feel we have done enough by reading and adopting the views expressed by the authors of articles and books, or simply by listening and adopting the views of those with whom we speak. And most of the time we are not even aware of how it all came about. We say, 'I think,' and don't realize that we are actually just paraphrasing our husbands, wives, or favorite columnists.

Since the subjects on which we feel we must have an "opinion" of our own are determined by outstanding events and trends, it is natural that the Germans should have become a problem regarding which no self-respecting individual may plead insufficient factual information and refuse to hand down a final verdict. After all: the Germans are, or at least are supposed to be, responsible for the latest world war which has engulfed most of the civilized countries. And today, when economic reasons make it advisable for the Western Allies to include part of the vanquished country in their program of rehabilitating Europe, it is these confounded "opinions" which create a climate of apology at home, of reluctance and half-heartedness abroad, hindering rather than advancing the giant task of getting mankind back to peaceful and civilized ways of life.

Books are one of the main sources for second-hand opinions. The better known and the more respected the author, the greater the influence of his opinions on the public. In connection with the Germans, one author has been instrumental in injecting into the minds of the American public some of his own personal resentment under the cover of objectivity and expert knowledge. He is Mr. Emil Ludwig. I am thinking in particular of that impressive-looking tome of his, *The Germans: Double History of a Nation,* which, though responsible for much anti-German opinion, is actually just so much bosh and poppycock.

Most of those who accept Mr. Ludwig's "historical proof" of the twofold character of the Germans, welcome it because it is grist on the mill of their own prejudices. Why should they doubt it?

It is so easy to forget that the twofold battle with good and evil is by no means a German monopoly but the very essence of humanity. Those who swallow Mr. Ludwig's "proofs" wholesale are not interested in discovering that the scientific garb in which he loves to clothe his hatred or his admiration is of a very precarious character. The fact that his relations to "Prussianism" have undergone an amazing change is quite revealing. In the beginning of the First World War, Mr. Ludwig published the most childish glorification of the "Fritz-spirit" (in his book, *Die Fahrten der Emden und der Ayesha*, Berlin, 1915). Yet when he did so, most of the "historical facts" used by him some thirty years later to prove the overall wickedness of the Germans, must have been well known to him as they were to most educated people all over the world.

Doubts as to the reliability of Mr. Ludwig's "historical proofs" become still more disturbing when one learns that for a while he claimed (and perhaps still does) to be the initiator of a new approach to the science of history. Indeed, he seriously proposed replacing "classical history" by a "poetical-intuitive approach." When one begins to realize that Mr. Ludwig's opinions on the Germans are those of a man who wantonly replaces hard facts by poetry and intuition, one's doubts as to the accuracy of his statements become downright alarming.

But who delves into an author's statements that way? Scarcely anyone. Probably no one. And the superficial manner in which the Ludwigs and their opinions have a way of coming up in idle conversation over a cocktail or after dinner or just before going to bed, leaves little possibility or desire for a more thorough investigation.

Mr. Ludwig says that the worst crime committed against the Germans after the last war was the League of Nations, an attempt to replace might by right in international affairs. In his judgment it was idle to try to supplant might by international law because the typical German mind is not open to such a step. Nor even, says Mr. Ludwig, do the Germans possess the sentiment upon which such a notion must rest.

Mr. Ludwig does not know or does not say that what is called international law is a very dubious matter. He does not know or does not say that up to 1919 might and its very expression and application, that is, war, was an essential part of that same international law, that it was a wholly lawful means of making foreign policy! Mr. Ludwig does not know or does not say that supplanting might by law, as undertaken by the League of Nations, simply meant taking the might away from the vanquished and keeping it solidly in the hands of the victors! Mr. Ludwig does not know or does not say that up to 1926 (the year of the admission of Germany to the League of Nations), the Germans had no possibility of participating in the substitution of law for might because they had been kept out of the Geneva setup. Mr. Ludwig does not know or does not say that the Germans are as law-abiding as any civilized people.

As for this matter of respect for the law, Mr. Ludwig, on the one hand, denies the Germans the quality outright and on the other hand ridicules them for possessing too much of it, going so far as to say that they stick to law even in making revolutions! Had Mr. Ludwig been interested in anything but voicing dangerously subjective opinions, he might have discovered that the German tragedy finds its most obvious explanation in that very attitude of civilized man's thirst for justice and reluctance to violate the law. Mr. Ludwig does not know or does not say that since there existed no lawful means of getting rid of that most vicious of dictatorships set up by the Nazis, the Germans suffered and hoped for help from the outside. Mr. Ludwig does not say—even though he must know—that the activities of the "Ludwigs" outside Germany contributed mightily to making this expectation on the part of the Germans vain. These Ludwigs obviously have little interest in elucidating problems objectively.

While the Ludwigs bitterly reproached the Germans because they fought, those same Ludwigs just as bitterly reproached the French because they did not fight. While the Ludwigs cried alarum when the French regime of Marshal Pétain dealt roughly with political adversaries, those same Ludwigs applauded a similarly ignominious procedure when it was applied by the de Gaulle committee in Algiers to officers of Marshal Pétain. Ludwigs foamed with indignation when British cities were bombed by the Germans; and they beamed with satisfaction when the same procedure was applied to German cities.

Beware of these molders of opinion! They cry out to the civilized world if hatred strikes *them!* Yet they cannot wait for the moment when hatred is exerted against those they hate. You may be sure that it is not the problems of mankind in which these Ludwigs are interested; what they are interested in is their personal problems. They are Hitlers in spirit. The only difference between them and the Austrian paperhanger is that Hitler really meant what he said.

2. What the Prosecution Forgot to Say

To visualize what actually happened in Germany, to understand how Nazism "befell" the Germans, we must bear in mind the basic likeness of the life of all mankind wherever and whenever it is organized in more or less civilized communities. This fundamental similarity is relevant for the understanding of the social conduct of any people, and it is rather surprising that precisely in judging the Germans these elementary things are so often left out of consideration.

All too often a number of superficial variants look like different fundamentals. Many observers and travelers have fallen dupes to this first-hand error and unintentionally become propagandists of half-truths. In addition to this the output of commercial word-sellers or news agents, who thrive

on a wholesale accentuation of the unusual, so in-
fluences the public's mind that these superficial
variants black out fundamental likenesses.

Whether the law of a land, that amazingly or-
derly labyrinth of rules and regulations prescribed
and maintained by authority for human action and
behavior, is written in English or German or French
or Spanish, is of little importance when viewed
against the fact that it is, in every civilized country,
the law and the effects its maintenance has exerted
on humans over long periods of time which make
people behave as members of organized communities.

Whether judges are elected to their office or
whether they are appointed civil servants is a matter
of secondary importance when viewed against the
common task of judges in all civilized countries,
which is to administer the law of their respective
lands.

Whether policemen wear fancy get-ups or military uniforms, whether they are Irish, Italian,
French, Jewish, German, or Anglo-Saxon, is immaterial when viewed against their universal as-
signment with which all members of all police
forces of all civilized countries of this world are
entrusted, the task of maintaining public order and
of enforcing regulations for the prevention and de-
tection of crime.

Whether the most important rules of law—the one which insures fulfillment of contractual obligations and the other which guarantees that what we earn or otherwise acquire belongs to us—are said to be instruments for the perpetuation of the Nazi State or whether they are considered the essential features of the capitalist system of free enterprise, is immaterial when viewed against the fact that they are, in the United States, in Great Britain, in Spain, in the countries of South America, or wherever you may care to focus your attention, not only the very basis of economic life, but that their maintenance is the very basis of Western civilization.

Whether Mr. Hitler was a skunk or Mr. Churchill an admirable knight in shining armor, whether Nero was a good fiddler or Napoleon an excellent mathematician, whether Mr. Roosevelt was a saint or Mr. Mussolini an inflated peacock is immaterial when viewed against the social functions they exerted during their time in public office. All held positions at the head of their respective organized communities. Sometimes such politicians turn out to be evil incarnate in the exercise of their social functions; sometimes they prove tolerably useful, but at all times civilized man must put up with them for the simple reason that they do a job which has to be done by someone.

Whether schools and universities are maintained by contributions of private citizens or whether the educational system is carried out with public funds is of secondary importance when viewed against the fact that in all civilized countries there are institutions of learning where young people become mentally equipped for the various tasks which life in complex communities reserves for persons equipped with a certain standard of education.

Whether the German is an accomplished goose-stepper, or the English Tommy an expert stiff-arm-swinger, or the French Blue Devil a snappy quick - short - stepper — parade specialties which make Americans smile as the more casual parade step of their own boys in uniform makes the British, French, and Germans smile—these constitute insignificant variants when viewed against the fact that all the boys are civilized men in uniform, drilled according to their country's rules in the military arts.

In connection with the Germans, the prosecutor has of course forgotten to tell the jury anything resembling the foregoing remarks; he has concentrated on the task of making the Germans appear as strange beasts, a cancer in the body of the civilized world. In the same vein he has insisted that Nazi theory springs straight from the roots of the utterly vicious German mind, that it is the very expression of the worst that Germany has produced, that is, of Prussianism. He has claimed that the Germans are responsible for Nazism, that it is thanks to their special type of slave mind and to their perverse masochistic tendencies that they craved the cracking of the Nazi whip over their own backs. He has led the jury to believe that the coming into power of Nazism is proof positive of the Germans' outspoken desire for domination.

Sometimes, I know, the prosecutor took pains to appear as an impartial observer by adding, with a condescending display of generosity, that the Germans have also produced a noteworthy number of the type of men who are considered the very ornament of humanity—musicians, writers, poets, thinkers, scientists, etc. But these were to be considered the product of "good Germany," a negligible portion of the population which, unfortunately indeed, is eternally subjugated by the evil forces which are said to represent the majority and which make this people the curse of the earth. Without them, the whole earth would be populated by law-abiding, peace-loving, generous, altruistic, civilized nations.

The way in which the prosecutor has presented the case, immediately betrays his endeavor to start out from what he would like to prove. He begins

33

with the opinion that the Germans are the curse of this earth and then proceeds to use wantonly selected facts to prove his opinion. It is hardly necessary for the defense to demonstrate the naïveté of such a method of "proving" pre-established opinions. It is precisely the method the Nazis used to prove conclusively that the British are the very curse of Europe and that the Americans are nothing but gangsters and racketeers. American non-gangsters and non-racketeers understand how absurd this is and that rejecting such "proofs" is about all one can do.

The Facts of the Matter

3. The Germans and the Nazi Struggle for Power

There is nothing simpler than hurling general accusations through space. This is the method the prosecution has chosen in the hope—borne out so far—of not being contradicted. However, when it is the relationship of a people to its political leadership which is involved and judged, such blanket accusations serve any number of purposes except that of finding out the truth. The reaction of a people, any people, to its political leadership cannot be fairly appraised without considering the course of the leaders' careers. Such a career is always divided into two phases: before accession to power and after. We are going to examine the accusations of the prosecution pertaining to the period when the Nazis were not yet in power but were struggling hard to attain it.

Who were they? A crowd of would-be office-holders of essentially the same type you find in any country, except that this group was in a state of extreme poverty. It was composed of an unemployed Austrian house-painter whose voice appealed to the masses, a few jobless ex-army officers like Goering and Roehm, a sadistically inclined school-teacher like the disgusting Streicher, a few lawyers without clients, some pitifully unsuccessful authors and journalists like Goebbels, and students like Hess who preferred beer cellars to the University and political chatter to study. Not a particularly representative group of Germans.

The fact that these miserable creatures made up their minds to go in for politics at a particularly propitious moment of general discontent is not particularly German either. Anyone in any country with a democratic constitution can choose his career, can he not? And anyone, in any country with a democratic constitution, can start a new party, can he not? Would it occur to anyone of sound mind to identify Mussert, the Dutch Nazi, or Degrelle, the Belgian Duce, or Quisling, the Norwegian *Gauleiter*, with the people among whom they were born and took up political activity?

Not only was there nothing specifically German about the initial group, but it included not one Prussian.

What did they actually do and say during the period of their struggle for power, that is, up to 1933? It is fairly simple to sum up what they said since all their words were based on one political textbook, Hitler's *Mein Kampf*. The fact that a man chose politics as his career at a certain moment in his life and formulated his ideas and his program in a book is not particularly German, or Prussian. Politicians all over the world have written programs and tried to sell their ideas to the public. Still, it could be that the ideas which this stepchild of nature formulated in his famous program were specifically German. Let us examine them.

We can start with what is considered the backbone of Nazi theory, the race concept. As expressed in *Mein Kampf*, this phony theory of a master race is definitely not German. The fathers of these ideas, which were taken up by Hitler and the few intellectuals who tried to give shape to his childish stammering, were the Frenchman, Comte Gobineau, and the Britisher, Houston Stewart Chamberlain.

Another of Hitler's "ideas" voiced in *Mein Kampf* is that of national unity. Is there anything specifically German about that? Is national unity not the very essence of all modern nations?

Is there anything specifically German about what is referred to as Hitler's originality in questions of political propaganda and mass psychology? His avowed models in these matters were none other than the British methods used during the First World War and the methods of Communist propaganda elaborated by Trotsky and applied by German Communists on orders from Moscow. As to his use of certain psychological tricks which may have been borrowed from the teachings of mass psychology, those who have ever so little knowledge of the subject and of the theoretical treatment it has received, know that the French physician, Gustave Le Bon, must be considered its father. The question has also been treated, more brilliantly than thoroughly, by Spanish theoreticians.

As to the introduction of certain methods employed in the political struggle for power as in vote-getting and the like, Hitler's indebtedness to Italian Fascism is obvious. The shirt nonsense, the salute, Hitler's title, etc., were all borrowed from the Fascist party of Signor Mussolini.

Whoever is able to distinguish between fact and fancy will fail to find anything specifically German in the whole pitiful collection of half-truths, borrowed ideas, and commonplaces which make up the Nazi bible *Mein Kampf*. Whoever knows even a little about the Germans, about their literature, their science, and especially their social sciences, must admit that the subject which has preoccupied the best German minds for centuries, that is, law and its significance for human life in society, plays no part in the masterpiece of ignorance and un-German pretensions in which an Austrian loud-speaker rambles on for pages on end about topics such as venereal diseases and the like. The utter disregard of *Mein Kampf* for law and its significance in social life at once brands Nazi theory as essentially un-German and essentially un-Prussian.

As I am speaking of what I know to be a strong feeling the Germans have for the law and its sacred inviolateness and of the preponderant place which the law has in the minds of the German people, I am reminded of a story which was a part of every German child's history lessons up to the time when the Nazis stole, swindled, and forced themselves into power and set out on their impossible attempt to wipe out a cultural development reaching back over centuries. It is the story of the miller of Potsdam and may well be called the German equivalent of the story of George Washington and the cherry tree.

Frederick the Great, one of the most powerful of Prussian kings, had erected the beautiful pleasure palace of *Sans Souci*. When he began living there he was bothered by the rattling of a windmill in the vicinity. He offered to buy the mill, but the miller refused to sell. It was his windmill, he said, as it had been his father's, and he meant to keep it and carry on his trade. The king resorted to pressure and even to threats. All to no avail. So the king had the miller appear before him. "I am the king," he said, "and I order you to give up your mill." "No, your Majesty," was the miller's reply, "you cannot order that as long as there is a supreme court in Berlin."

The king is said to have received this answer with great delight; the mill still stands and has become a shrine and a symbol for the ideals of law and justice.

I remember having been at *Sans Souci* twice as a child, once with my parents and again with my history professor. The impression I carried away had nothing to do with the magnificence of the palace but to this day is linked with the story of the miller and his trust in justice. I believe it illustrates how completely un-German the Nazi theory or rather practice of lawlessness is.

Who can wonder that practically no one in Germany, or outside the country for that matter, took this "Nazi stuff" seriously until the day, alas too late, when the Nazi gangsters had entrenched themselves solidly in positions of power.

I have tried to show that the struggle of the Nazi gang for public support cannot be considered es-

pecially German, that it is the game of politicians
the world over in any country with a democratic
constitution. That the Nazis formed a party in order
to obtain a nucleus of active supporters is also the
game of politicians in any and every country of the
world. That they found people at home and abroad
who, for various personal reasons, gave them financial support happens to political parties the
world over. That they held political rallies to get
votes? That they used propaganda? That they
promised everything to everyone? It would be in-
sane to label any of these methods distinctively
German.

Proofs against the senselessness of the opinion
which identifies Nazis with Germans and Prussians are unlimited. One of the best-known ex-
pressions of that opinion is the one concerned with
brutality. It runs like this: Prussianism is equivalent
to brutality; Nazism is the very expression of brutality; consequently Nazism equals Prussianism.
One of those logical-sounding proofs . . . but
only for those who do not realize the danger of
playing with syllogisms, only for those who do not
recognize that the Nazi-Prussian argument stands
and falls with the premise. And the premise is an
assumption, as unfounded as the Nazi assumption
that Jews are scoundrels and the consequent argument: you are a Jew; therefore: you are a scoun-

drel. Of course, in neither of these cases is it difficult to find a number of examples to support the premise. There are brutes among Germans and scoundrels among Jews, just as there are brutes and scoundrels in all countries the world over. It is simple indeed to suppress the fact, by not mentioning it, that in both our cases the overwhelming majority of Germans and Jews are plain, honest, law-abiding, civilized people.

As for the Prussianism-equals-brutality myth, it cannot be stated too often that the Nazi gang was not composed of Prussians; that Prussians were conspicuously absent in the entire Nazi setup; that the only attempt made by the Nazis to get into power by a *coup d'état* (the use of brute force, back in 1923) failed pitifully; and, finally, that if the premise in question were true, one would have to explain away that the whole Nazi business was staged by an Austrian, that it started in Southern Germany, and that Prussia was that part of Germany which withstood the ruthless propaganda onslaughts of the Nazis longer than did any other part of the country. Presumably clever people sometimes say that the strong and powerful socialist pre-von Papen Prussian government could easily have disposed of Hitler and his gang and that the fact they did not is an indication of their desire to be ruled by the Nazis, specifically by the Austrian corporal.

I happen to be a Prussian and I think I know what it is to have a feeling for the law, and so I make bold to tell you that the Prussian socialists in government did not attempt to dispose of the Hitler gang and its helpers by brute force because such methods would have been illegal and contrary to the democratic constitution. They would, in all probability, have provoked civil war. The Prussian government would not use what thoughtless and misinformed people call "Prussian methods." Not that they stood by idly. What they did was to go to court. That did not stop Hitler; but it is important to know about it, for it belongs to the realm of facts which opinion-mongers carefully avoid so as to be able to offer the gullible public enticing formulas which make for hatred, hatred to which so many hitch their personal bandwagon.

If the Prussianism-equals-brutality premise were more than a myth, more than a saga dished out by a few so-called intellectuals, partly in order to hide from themselves and from others their own shortcomings, partly because they think they have found an easy and comfortable way of disposing of their personal grievances and resentment on the backs of voiceless and defenseless millions, if this premise were more than a myth, it would also have to be true that the land of Prussia is the very homestead of anarchy where brutes using brute force fight each other like wild beasts. But I think people in general know, even if they know little else about Prussia, that it has always been the land of law and order *par excellence*. It is a well-known fact that modern economic life went on in Prussia because people kept their word and paid their debts; that the administration of justice lay in the hands of judges who, though not high-salaried, were known to be the least corruptible. The qualities of the members of the Prussian public administration have been cited often enough. And Prussian officials had very limited authority as far as the private lives of citizens were concerned. It was, moreover, the duty of special courts to see to it that any misuse of their power be examined and reprimanded forthwith.

Before winding up what I consider important to throw a light of fairness on the most prevalent of the senseless opinions circulated on the German people, let me add a few words on the death of the German Republic which agonized all through the hectic year of 1932.

It was in 1932 that the repercussions of the economic world crisis which had started in the United States in 1929 struck Germany. It struck particularly hard because of Germany's economic weakness. Not only was the vast majority of the population living in appalling misery, but the country was seething with political unrest. It was in that same year of 1932 that Hitler was naturalized in Germany (not by Prussia but by the State of Brunswick) so that he might be able to run for the office of President. He did run and was beaten by Hindenburg who, in the minds of the majority of the Germans, occupied a place similar to that which another great soldier occupied in the minds of a considerable number of Frenchmen under German occupation, similar to the place which other great soldiers have occupied in the past and are occupying today in the minds of citizens of various countries.

One major election followed another. None of them resulted in a clear-cut majority in Parliament on which a government might securely have based its position. Effective obstruction was carried on in friendly collaboration by Nazis and Communists.

The election decreed by von Papen, then Chancellor, brought about a serious Nazi defeat which, in its turn, gave new impetus to activities aimed at a defensive and offensive coalition between Socialists and Communists. General von Schleicher formed a government, and it was here that took shape the queerest part of the agony of the German Repub-

lic, the intrigues around Hindenburg. They were
maneuvered chiefly by von Papen who succeeded
in convincing the aged *Reichspräsident* that he
should drop von Schleicher and, in spite of his disgust for the Austrian corporal, entrust Hitler, the
nominal head of the strongest party, with the for-
mation of the government by naming him Chancellor.

That a few von Papens existed in Germany and
jumped at the possibility of playing the fascinating
game of politics at the expense of the exhausted
German people cannot be construed as a reproach
to this people. Rather should it call for compassion.
One might as well blame a whole people for an infinitesimal percentage of gangsters and criminals.
Or laud an entire population for a few thinkers,
poets, musicians, movie stars. . . . What was actually happening was that all the members of a former
ruling group had decided not to "die" and were ly-
ing in wait for an opportunity to win back some of
their former glamor. You need but think of France
to recall that there, too, a fairly sizable number
of such good-for-nothing diehards who had never
ceased living in the past were craving to re-establish
their vanished importance and to resume a regretted
and cherished busy idleness at the expense of the
people.

The support von Papen managed to eke out

was negligible, especially in Prussia. When Hitler formed his first cabinet the von Papen crowd, far from seeking to identify themselves with the Nazis, tried to fool them and use them as a means of "liberating the country" from the danger of people whose avowed goal was to overthrow the system of private property and enterprise. Unfortunately for them, and more particularly for the German people, instead of fooling the Nazis, they themselves were the ones to be thoroughly fooled.

The hope of the Nazis to set up their dictatorship legally by getting the necessary majority of votes had failed. The story of how the Nazis swindled and elbowed themselves into power by falsehood, deceit, and acts of appalling illegality (of which the *Reichstag* fire and the infamous *Ermächtigungsgesetz* were the most important), has been told often enough and need not be repeated here. Let me recall, however, that it was the *Ermächtigungsgesetz* by means of which Nazi fanatics, with the help of the votes of deadly frightened burghers, literally handed over to Hitler's gang the fate of the German people. It was this coalition, born of red terror, which permitted those unscrupulous Nazi scoundrels to drape themselves in pseudo-legality and start applying their *Fauna-Weltanschauung* to the "management of public affairs."

The fact remains, however, that in the last free elections 33% of the votes were actually cast for the Nazis. Is it possible to identify this percentage of Germans with the Hitler gang? It is of course easy to say that all the things which the Nazis promised they would do, once they were in power, succeeded in bringing to the surface the beastly instincts they evoked in their voters. But anyone who has watched the Nazi voters knows that the majority of them fell for bait which was anything but an appeal to beastly instincts. They fell for things of which no honest man in the world need be ashamed: patriotism and revolt against injustice. That they lacked comprehension and foresight is another story. But it is obvious that they fell for clever propaganda, the propaganda that harped on the shortcomings of parliamentary democracy.

Still other Nazi voters were influenced by propaganda which branded the democratic regime with having introduced the spoils system in Germany's public life. Is it so difficult to understand that certain Germans manifested their disgust at seeing public office handed out to party members, by casting their votes for politicians who promised to abolish such an unsavory system? It must not be forgotten that the Germans were accustomed, as far back as their memories could reach, to seeing public administration in the hands of a Civil Service chosen solely on the basis of qualification, and that they were opposed to favoritism and all the iniquities it entails.

There were still others who fell for propaganda which pointed a finger at the flagrant incapacity of post-war democracy to cope with the millions of unemployed and the consequent social disease from which Germany was suffering. Germany's real difficulties sprang from the wanton curtailment of German foreign trade which cannot be attributed to a lack of the country's main raw materials, the people's hands, brains, or their desire to work. I have seen no civilized people work harder than the Germans for less compensation. But even the Germans cannot eat iron and coal.

One can produce commodities out of iron and coal and sell them to others who produce other necessities of life, and buy their goods in return. But if this essential procedure is wantonly curtailed, as it was after the first World War, because of senseless opinions circulated about the German people, can one blame that people for revolting against injustice? The German people, like all the other peoples of this earth, want to live. And anyone who has lived among them knows their stubborn *Fleiss*, their will to overcome difficulties. Only lunatics and those who, for reasons of personal hatred or self-interest, try to fool other people, can persist in the infamous legend of Germany's and especially Prussia's thirst for domination. And when this accusation is hurled at Germany by members of a nation which has, in fact, dominated the world for centuries, it carries with it a note of comic absurdity which cannot fail to bring an understanding smile to the faces of those who take the trouble to think.

The *Lebensraum* or place-in-the-sun slogan met with sympathy in still other Nazi voters. It was not because of their thirst for domination but because of a very human need to find a way out of misery, a way out of a situation into which French and British politicians in power during the last post-war period had placed a most unfortunate people. Try for a moment to picture eighty million human beings crowded into some 200,000 square miles, and then consider, by way of comparison, that thirty-one million people, for instance, populating four parts of the British Commonwealth (Australia, New Zealand, Canada, and South Africa) have 7,500,000 square miles at their disposal. This comparison alone might actually make one wonder why only 33% of the Germans fell for the *Lebensraum* propaganda of the Nazis! The common man in Germany, the one we are interested in, never gave so much as a fleeting thought to world domination. He thought, and thinks, only of working hard enough to make a decent living—which is the aim of the common man the world over.

Perhaps these few reminders will show that it was human, not vicious, for 33% of the Germans to have cast their votes for political scoundrels who took advantage of their misery and their patriotism.

And if it is said that only the Germans could have produced as wicked a crowd as the Nazis, it is easy to counter by saying that such asocial elements as the Nazi gang are to be found in any people, anywhere, and there is no need to delve into history to prove it. Politicians with so-called Fascist tendencies are a normal occurrence in all countries, and you need only picture a civilized people living through Germany's last post-war period to realize that, given a similar set of external circumstances, such adventurers might have come to the surface anywhere, and their struggle for power might have succeeded in much the same way as Nazi alchemy succeeded in Germany.

Or again, is it specifically German that a small number of professional soldiers favored the Nazis' rise to power? Hardly, for anyone must know that a very obvious kinship exists between the ideals of Fascist politicians and the military profession. The former aim at commanding a nation; the latter are trained to command people in uniform. In so far as Germany is concerned, the only hope some ex-army people had of retrieving their lost glamor lay in Nazi success. The presence of such adventurers was more noticeable in Germany than in other countries because the authorized 100,000-man army of post-war Germany was unable to absorb all of them and there was not the alternative of using them, as other countries did, for administering conquered countries and populations controlled by a motherland.

One of the most flaunted "opinions" about Germany concludes that Nazism must be the very expression of the most cherished concepts of at least 33% of the German voters and those representatives of the burgher parties who cast their votes for them because, so the argument runs, this part of the people must have known what the Nazis were up to since their program had been widely diffused and their propagandists had often enough stated that the party would stick to its program. On examination, such an argument falls to pieces just as the others we have examined.

Parliamentary democracy with which highly idealistic politicians of post-war Germany had blessed the German people and which, boiled down to its essentials, was the introduction of a certain manner of selecting the men who would fulfill political functions in the social life of the country, had not only aroused the common man's suspicion of politicians but had thoroughly acquainted him with the meaning of campaign promises. Can the inevitable consequences of democracy serve as a basis for condemning the German people?

This tendency to be suspicious of politicians, of harboring even a certain contempt for them, exists wherever a similar mode of selecting political leadership exists. It was certainly the case in France. It was and is the case in Great Britain. It is so much the case in Great Britain that H. G. Wells, whose disgust with the political leadership of his country was common knowledge, actually received a certain response to his vigorous advocacy of a new method of selection directed towards a "non-party administration of public affairs." It is the case in the United States. A recent survey by the National Opinion Research Center of the University of Denver on the attitude of the American voter towards politicians revealed the following: seven voters out of ten would not like to see a son of theirs go into politics; 50% of the voters questioned thought it practically impossible for a man to remain honest once he entered politics. Is it not fair then to say that many Germans who cast their votes for the Nazis, voted for men who had promised to abolish this profession?

If, from the fact that 33% of the voters cast their votes for the Nazi party, one deduces that all those jobless, idealistic, befuddled, or frightened burghers who made up these voters and those re-actionaries who helped them along, did so because they craved the crimes and mismanagement the Nazis committed in their revolting misuse of the legal-political apparatus, one attributes more fore-sight to these people than to far better informed political leaders of France and England! No one in the world expected the Nazis to do what politi-cians are not expected to do, what they never do, that is, live up to campaign promises and threats.

Perhaps the most significant illustration of this is what former French Premier Daladier said after Hitler had come to power. He was asked what he thought of Hitler's foreign policy program as outlined in *Mein Kampf*. "But do you believe," Daladier is said to have replied, "that a policy can be made according to a book?" And then he added: "I am a practical politician and I assure you that there is no chance in the world that Hitler will fol-low his book. Reality will teach him."

No one person could ever attempt to refute all the rubbish that has been thrown at the public by the most varied crowd of self-appointed prosecu-tors. But I do believe, Members of the American Jury, that I have shown conclusively that a sizeable number of the flippant accusations hurled against my people by an overzealous prosecution dissolve into smoke as soon as one examines facts and looks reality in the face. Perhaps I could have been still more conclusive in my explanation of the actions and reactions of the Germans when faced with the most determined efforts of a tightly knit group of political activists bent on acceding to power whatever the cost. I could have drawn parallels to past and present demagogues and would-be Hitlers in action all over the world, to people who shout and sing and moan and groan at masses brought together by some real or illusory common grievance, who promise and threaten, who organize and collect money—in order to get votes. And finally, I could have drawn your attention to the fact that right here in the United States there is a fairly general positive response to the idea of having Communists put out of circulation, and also to the execution of that idea.

However, my purpose is not to present an address on politics. I took up my pen for the defense of my people in misery and despair, to refute a number of cheap and false accusations which have been more or less skilfully instilled into your minds and which, since they are untrue, cannot serve any fair-minded person as a basis for escape into the comfortable conclusion: "The Germans are getting only what is coming to them."

4. The Germans and History

The importance of the historical argument in support of all the evil things said and circulated about the Germans is evident when one realizes: first, that the French prosecutor's chief refrain of "three wars made by Germany during the last seventy-five years" constitutes a basis for the overall rather harmful official French attitude of obstructionism in peace policies since V-J Day, and second, that any reference to this refrain is always taken up with gleeful haste by those who see their advantage in going to bat in the role of prosecutor in the German case. Beyond this there are quite a number of more or less idiotic opinions about the Germans, and especially the Prussians, which are based less on first-hand knowledge and experience than on historical hearsay picked up in history lessons and from history books.

All right then. What about this historical business? What about all that has been written by men who "know" their history, who have delved deep down into the past, who go back to the opinions of Tacitus on the Germans and the Prussians (why not?), who have dug up scores of historical facts which all seem to corroborate the premise that the Germans, and especially the Prussians, are a thoroughly wicked people, vicious in the extreme, living only in preparation of the moment when they can try, with some chance of success, to subjugate other nations; that they are curiously dual in their mental constitution, lazy and covetous of the labor of others, arrogant and always relying on brute force. And after all, and this we hear practically every day, during the last seventy-five years they have invaded France three times. And didn't they fight like lions in this last war? Well then, what about history?

This history question is a serious one indeed. And it is of great personal interest to me for it instantly brings to my mind the questions I started asking myself the very day I set foot on French soil after having turned my back on the Nazi regime in 1936. For I had had history lessons, too; I, too, had studied history books. General history, as you learned it, as I learned it, and as most people learn it, is and always has been, as far as foreign peoples are concerned, quite a superficial thing. You remember as well as I do that it was limited to a general outline of the internal political development of foreign countries (rulers and forms of government), to wars and their apparent consequences, to dates—all of it seasoned with a few sidelights on the "outstanding features" of a people one knew only by hearsay and through the medium of what one was told about them. "History" usually stopped with a few notes in a last chapter entitled: "Up to the Present Time." The present time not yet being "history," it played a minor role in history lessons—it was left to the newspapers.

I often wonder how many people have thought, after learning scores of "historical facts" about a foreign people, how strange it is that we should be able to know what *was* without knowing what *is*.

Specifically now: it is quite possible that a person has learned "all about German history" and still knows nothing whatever about the Germans. If we are honest with ourselves we will admit that our knowledge of the past is exclusively of a second-hand nature, that it springs solely from what others have said and have written down. And how can conclusions from documents and contemporary opinions be reasonably considered proof of what we "know," since these documents and opinions are the very source of our knowledge? By accepting them we start from what we are told has been, and then we apply a ready-made scheme to what is. Has it never occurred to you that if we really want to know, if we really want to try to find out, it might be wiser to start with what is and then, cautiously, try to step back in search for the truth of what was?

Think of the possibility (even though it is a fairly remote one) that someone, some 1800 years hence, is going to dig up Mr. Ludwig's book on the Germans and will try to "learn" from Mr. Ludwig what "was"!!! And although I believe it is fairly improbable, it should not be difficult to visualize such a possibility when today we see a Mr. Nizer, a New York attorney and author of *What To Do With Germany*, starting his series of "historical proofs" of the criminal character of the Germans by presenting opinions of Tacitus, that old chatterbox!

Needless to say, that kind of historian and that type of history exists in Germany too. They "prove" in a similar manner that the British have been and are at the root of every European war during the last three centuries. They bolster such "proof" with documents and opinions. "History," after all, is a treasure house of all sorts of "facts" which support whatever one wishes to prove.

But now let us look at the three wars "made in Germany" during the last seventy-five years. Why does one choose precisely seventy-five years of history? It seems so arbitrary. If the prosecution had chosen one hundred and forty years, for instance, we would find ourselves right in the era of the Napoleonic wars, face to face with a situation which would not look too good for the French.

In order to give the prosecution some of their own medicine in their shortsighted, dangerous, and superficial attempt to blame the Germans for all the evils which have befallen this world in the wake of wars and their aftermath, let me quote a few figures. In a table representing a summary of the part played by important states in the wars of modern times over a period reaching from 1480 to 1941, Prof. Quincy Wright of the University of Chicago (*A Study of War*, II vol., 1552 p., 1942) shows that Great Britain leads the field with participation in 78 wars; next comes France with 71; in the third place we find Spain with 64; fourth runner-up is Russia with 61; fifth-place honors go to the Empire (Austria) with 52; and—believe it or not, but these are the facts as gathered by Professor Wright and his collaborators—Prussia (Germany) is in a draw with the Netherlands with a poor 23.

To be fair, one must point out that Prussia and thereafter Germany were relative late-comers on the international scene. For this reason and also because it may be of interest to see what the American record looks like, I narrowed the field to the period from 1750 to 1941. And these are the results: Great Britain again leads with 41 wars; France again takes second place with 33; Prussia-Germany runs third with 14, with the United States a close runner-up with 13.

And still, seventy-five, one hundred and forty, four hundred and sixty, two hundred and ninety years or any similarly limited period must appear a precarious stretch of time when one thinks of the hundreds of thousands of years which represent the development of the human species in its various forms.

But notwithstanding my doubts as to the usefulness of such an arbitrary choice, and because I know people are interested right now in the wars "made in Germany" and not in those attributed to other countries, let us take up the last seventy-five years. I understand that most of you "learned European history" from Robinson and Beard's *Outlines of European History*. At the time you were studying, it is likely that a last chapter dealing with the first

World War had been added to the deadweight of "historical facts." You learned that after the assassination of the successor to the throne of "Austria" by a Serbian patriot, "Austria" exacted quite a number of things from "Serbia" in order to secure reparation for such an offense. You learned that it was clear that "Russia" would not stand by and see "Serbia" conquered by "Austria." You then learned that "Germany" would aid "Austria" in every way if she were attacked by "Russia," that "Germany" wanted "Serbia" punished and "was willing to risk a world war to have her desire," that "Austria" declared war on "Serbia," that "Russia" mobilized, that "Germany" declared war on "Russia," then on "Belgium" and "France," and so on and so forth.

This became your knowledge as it did many other people's, and it all was served with the usual anti-Prussian trimmings. Did you not, for instance, learn that it was "Prussia" which introduced the new principle of the "nation in arms," whereas war, in the past, had been the business of "professional soldiers?" Actually Prussian war-mindedness was born when Prussia was aching under the heel of the victorious armies of Napoleon the Great and as a dismal consequence of that period.

I think I can easily predict what our children and our children's children will learn about this most recent war once a new chapter has been added to Robinson and Beard's *Outlines of European History*. The new chapter will sound uncannily like the one you studied after the last war.

Mention will be made of the fact that a new manifestation of Prussianism took the particularly hideous form of Nazism; that in the midst of a peace-loving world, war-thirsty Nazi-Prussian Germany was burning with impatience to go to war again; that after having heavily rearmed, "Germany," on the most ridiculous and shameful pretext, fell upon "Poland"; that "Germany," having been warned by "France" and "Great Britain" of the consequences of such an attack, proved once more her insatiable desire to demonstrate her superiority to the world by a new war; that "France" and "Great Britain" declared war on her "for the defense of justice against brute force," etc., etc. I have purposely not mentioned the "cause of Poland" in my predictions on the new chapter because what is said on the "cause of Poland" will depend on what Allied statesmen will do on behalf of Poland in the peace to come. If "Russia" has her way, things will sound different than if "Poland" recovers her pre-war territory.

In this connection I must call attention to a very curious phenomenon. While things were happening, while the infernal, beastly business of fighting, killing, and destroying was engulfing the greater part of this world and affecting millions of people who never had done any harm to one another, while it was bringing sorrow and suffering to countless individuals on all sides, we were, in a certain measure, differentiating between those who were actually responsible for what was going on and those who were mere tools of slaughter.

In so far as Germany was concerned, we heard about the German people and their fighting qualities, we heard about the Nazi rulers, we heard about the terror regime of the Gestapo, about concentration camps, *Waffen* SS, *Gauleiters*, Quislings, Goebbels' propaganda, etc.

Very soon after the fighting war was over and belonged to the past, albeit the immediate past, a curious thing happened: all differentiation ceased and in its stead we heard only of "Germany," the "Aggressor," responsible for having plunged mankind into a new world war, and deserving of appropriate punishment; "Germany" the criminal, to be chained or crippled or treated in keeping with "her" crime.

Does it not seem curious that what *is*, that what we observe today or what we observed yesterday happening under our very eyes should undergo so amazing a change the red-hot second it belongs to the past, were this past but a day old?

We know today that it was not "Germany" which was doing things but some eighty million helpless individuals trapped in the grip of a political regime of bloody terror and held under the special ruling of army regulations. We know that German generals did things, that Nazi politicians did things, that officials did things, that innumerable Germans in arms did things (most unpleasant things, to be sure, as has been the rule for the people-in-arms, the common-man-in-arms as far back as history goes), but no actual "Germany" was active.

And yet, today people say that "Germany" has done all this! In history books we will read of those "great actors of history," those *"dramatis personae* on the international stage"—"Germany," "Russia," the "United States," "Great Britain." Politicians will carry on, believing themselves to be, and looked upon as being, representatives of those mysterious international entities. They will conclude treaties for all those *"dramatis personae* on the international stage," and they will try to enact a system for enforcing the peace among the "national entities."

Did it ever occur to you to ask yourself the very serious question as to why it is that the mere fact that events have happened, that they belong to the

past and therefore belong to history, has the amazing consequence of making mysterious "entities"
suddenly come to the surface?

I for one have been haunted by this question
ever since the dismal abyss existing between what
is taught in universities and what goes on in real
life struck me, and this is what I found: that in
reality such a thing as "Germany" or "France" or
the "United States" or "Great Britain" simply does
not exist. I sharpened my wits and used the means
of observation with which we are all endowed, and
wherever I looked, whatever I saw, at no time did
I behold one of the "Great Powers." I saw people.
I observed legal mechanisms in action. I watched
politicians in office. I observed everything that
constitutes and makes possible mankind's life in
organized society. I watched individuals act and I
examined their thoughts. I saw them animated by
certain ideas and trying to attune their activities to
their ideas. But always they were persons, human
beings, and all much the same. But I never saw
"Germany" or "France" or the "United States" or
"Great Britain" except in history books, in books
on international law, in books on international relations, in books on international politics and referred to in speeches by politicians.

I tried to inform myself further by a serious study
of hundreds of works by men who had explored

social facts "scientifically." In all my studies of this subject I found only one person, a German law professor, who maintained that he had beheld such a mysterious entity with his very own eyes, "proving" in this way the real existence of this phenomenon. But no one else has, and we may presume that this gentleman was in a trance.

The master-minds of international law, of international relations, and of international politics, as well as all the experts on history, are always satisfied to start their reflections with the completely arbitrary supposition that such mysterious entities, international personalities, or whatever they call them, do exist, without bothering to question their premise. A few less complacent minds calm their doubts with one of two explanations: either they admit that these mysterious entities are simplifications which make the difficulties of exploring mankind's life in society easier, or they call them "juridical persons" and let it go at that.

Skepticism towards traditional thinking is fortunately gaining ground and today the "scientific" attitude in this question holds that the concept of "national entities acting in the international field" is a fiction. A fiction cannot suffer from hunger; only people can and do.

5. The Germans Under the Nazis in Power

The opinion-mongers who set such great store by the slogan of "the three wars 'made in Germany' within the last seventy-five years," cannot be expected to abandon their case even though we have shown that their cherished premise dissolves in thin air under less biased or uncritical scrutiny. They contend that the behavior of the German people after the Nazi accession to power was so completely in keeping with that premise that it must be sound after all; that there must be something fishy about an argument which seems to explode it. Nothing is truer than the old adage: A man convinced against his will is of the same opinion still . . .

So, Members of the American Jury, let us examine the behavior of the Germans under the Nazis through uncolored glasses, and in order to avoid the ever-present danger of false analogies, let us begin by stressing the marked difference between the legal-political organization constituting the framework of communal life among the Anglo-American peoples and that of the peoples not only of Germany but of the entire European continent.

In the United States the administration of justice consists essentially in that the interpretation and adaptation, the preservation and rejuvenation of the rules of law lie in the hands of judges who are elected, whereas the Germans, as most Europeans, have for long centuries entrusted their well-being to legislatures speaking through statutes.

Furthermore, again in contrast to conditions in the United States, the management of public affairs in the countries of Europe is largely the business of trained civil servants who are not elected but who are selected and appointed on the basis of qualification and merit.

Both these points are vitally important. They are characteristic of the management of public affairs all over the European continent, as well in regard to public administration in general as to the administration of justice in particular. They go back to Roman law, and far from being a German specialty in either form or origin, constitute one of the most interesting aspects of the long drawn-out cultural conquest of Central Europe by the lingering tradition of classical antiquity.

The details of these differences between the Anglo-American and Continental European systems matter as little at this time as a comparison of their respective merits and demerits. Both systems have their advantages and drawbacks. What is important to understand, is that the drawbacks of the European system are precisely what made it possible in Germany for a gang of ruthless politicians to "seize power" in the nick of time and to carry out their partially sinister, partially senseless activity. When you hear or read certain current opinions on the Germans—such as the one which refers to their servile submission to the "authorities," their docile acceptance of statutes even when such statutes clash with their individual sense of justice and fairness, or that other opinion which maintains that all German judges and public officials must be considered convinced Nazis because they applied and executed the legal rules and regulations enacted by the Nazi government—when you hear such opinions, you naturally associate the terms "judge" and "public official" with the type of men who hold corresponding positions in your country.

In so doing, and because you do not realize the fundamental difference between the situation of judges and public officials in America and that of men who held such positions in Germany, you draw unfounded inferences. You do so because, in your mind, they seem to be the only possible explanation of the fact that German judges applied, along with the bulk of the law, some especially hideous flowers of Nazi legal wisdom which those scoundrels had incorporated in the law of the country. The seemingly compelling character of such a conclusion dwindles away the very moment one realizes that judges in Germany are civil servants paid for carrying out, to the best of their ability, the job of applying and executing the laws enacted by the legislator.

There is, however, a much more arresting and convincing way of disproving the opinion which maintains that German judges proved themselves fervent adherents of Nazi theory, when they continued to perform their job of applying the law of the country after it had become perverted by the inclusion of statutes enacted by the Nazi government. It is this: that the Nazi regime, fully aware of the fact that German judges would not be willing or obedient instruments for the illegal maintenance of Nazi dictatorship, set up special "courts" to deal with political adversaries and with those who dared to utter a word of disapproval or disgust. These were the so-called people's courts— "courts" in name only, for their panel of five judges comprised only two professionals, the other three (constituting the majority) being chosen from among high-ranking members of the Nazi hierarchy.

In so far as the common man, the German John Doe, and his fate are concerned, the coming into power of the Nazis was the beginning of enslavement, of wanton disregard of age-old guarantees of personal and individual liberty, of the introduction into German public life of the most amazing system of organized corruption and immorality, of reckless exploitation of public office for personal profit, of appalling abuse of power and revolting disregard of the common interest, all for the sake of the achievement of "political" aims born and reared in the heads of ignoramuses, of people who knew of the joys and sorrows of the life of the common man by hearsay only. And it all came to a head through shrewd criminal treason against the all too credulous Germans, finally dragged into this war by promises of peace in honor and justice, led to death and destruction by a gang of fanatics who, still not satisfied with having achieved their selfish aims by their victory over the German people and the maintenance of an unheard-of reign of terror within Germany, turned against the world in an attempt to gratify their insatiable ambition.

But how was all that possible? How was it possible that the world stood by complacently, while in the course of the first six years of their rule, from 1933 to 1939, the Nazis cajoled or forced an entire nation along the road of its martyrdom? In contrast to many sensational writers on the subject, I do not believe that a detailed description and enumeration of Nazi crimes and misdeeds can serve to answer that question. The lurid portrayal of abnormality and moral deformation can scarcely provide a basis for the condemnation of a whole people. The approach to social questions from an individual angle must of necessity be grossly misleading. In questions of social relevance, the individual make-up, motives and standards of those fulfilling socially important functions in a given society have little to do with the beneficial or disastrous effects of their actions. There is little doubt that those men and women who advocated and enacted the Eighteenth Amendment to the American Constitution, were animated by the purest motives and goaded to take their stand by the most elevated moral and ethical principles. But this legislation produced a most disastrous and disruptive effect on American life and has left its scars long after its final repeal.

If the Nazis-equal-Germans myth contained so much as an inkling of truth, the Nazis would scarcely have felt compelled to create and continue to expand (in addition to the maintenance of the normal legal mechanism) a complicated party apparatus and an army of hundreds of thousands of Gestapo men. Nor would they have considered it necessary to have their Gestapo henchmen perpetrate their sinister misdeeds under cover of darkness so as not to arouse the people.

Can one be blind to the point of not realizing that a heavily armed Gestapo officer for every hundred Germans was not put in his job as living evidence of the love of the Germans for the Nazi regime? Can one be blind to the point of not seeing that the hundreds of thousands of Germans who were murdered or thrown into concentration camps were not dealt with in such a summary fashion for having expressed acceptance of the Nazi regime? Can one be blind to the point of not seeing that the valiant guardians of both the Catholic and Protestant faiths were persecuted because of their resistance to the Nazis' attempt to replace Christian faith by a pitifully primitive mythology?

If the prosecution maintains that those who did manifest resistance against the Nazis represent but a very small minority and cannot be regarded as an asset for the overwhelming majority of the Germans, we may suggest that this type of argument works both ways, and that the small minority of scoundrels, political gangsters, profiteers, and intellectual hoodlums which made up the Nazis in government and the SS leaders behind them can scarcely be identified with the majority of the Germans either.

But let us now look at what happened to the common German, how Nazism actually "happened" to him, let us consider what the Nazis did to my people, to those thousands and thousands of decent families, to their friends and relatives, to all those unsuspecting people who had neither time for nor any special interest in permanent concern with politics, who bore the hardships of everyday life with admirable fortitude, with unflinching courage and hope for a better future, who longed for music, for a game of cards with friends, for a game of skittles, a visit to relatives, a meeting in the good old *Verein*, who dressed neatly in Sunday clothes each week, who preferred the *Gemütlichkeit* of their family parties to rabble-rousing politics, who liked to add a note of gaiety to their reunions with friends and relatives by serving home-brewed currant wine, who could not and would not judge public affairs from any point of view other than that of their own personal life, who were told that it was their duty to vote and who did so, who believed what was printed in the newspapers because it was printed in the newspapers, to whom the suppression of unrestrained political liberties meant little because the introduction of those same liberties had not bettered their lot and had brought about the disruptive and futile bickerings of a multitude of parties and the specter of civil war and revolution, in short to the plain common man who makes the world go round and who represents the backbone of every civilized country in the world . . . and who is "getting it" now because he "accepted and tolerated" the Nazis!

After the hectic year of 1932, the year of the agony of the German Republic, the year during which the country was in a state verging on permanent civil war, with millions of unemployed, with widespread misery, with the danger of a Communist uprising garishly and cleverly publicized, the common man in Germany felt actually relieved when this new party came into power. It should not be difficult to understand that a population which had been called to take part in six major elections in one year under the most hectic circumstances should feel relieved at the idea of having a stable government which was promising to better the general conditions of the country. When the house is on fire, the fire chief takes over and everyone knows this must be so to avert catastrophe. It should not be difficult to understand such a reaction on the part of a population which, during thirteen years of parliamentary democracy and its consequent vote-getting activities, had become accustomed to the idea of hearing politicians promise all sorts of things, even evil things, and of seeing them, once in power, simply fulfilling the functions of government and forgetting all about campaign promises.

Here we must recall what I said a few pages ago about the fundamental differences in the systems of public administration in America and Europe. Prussia, the biggest German state, had been administered by its traditional Civil Service of great efficiency and great integrity even under the Weimar socialists who, in spite of their theoretical proclamations of a social revolution with the consequent upheaval of the whole economic system, had done a fairly good job of governing, a job which will be remembered in Germany in a rather positive way once the Nazi crowd is forgotten and its mismanagement of public affairs remains only as an example of how things should not be done.

It was natural that a people which had gone through this experience and was tired of political strife, should expect that the Nazis would, in so far as threats and promises were concerned, do what the others had done, that is, forget them. What they did hope for was that the Nazis would better their general condition. And being worn out by politics, they adopted a wait-and-see attitude when the Nazis set out to govern the country. Seemingly it was an innocent beginning.

As you look at the picture I am trying to paint, you must realize how diabolically unfair it is to look back and watch from a perfectly safe vantage point outside the danger zone and with a comfortable space of time in between, how all the evils which started with the Nazis' coming into power in Germany were "accepted" by the Germans and then to proceed and to blame the Germans for having "accepted" them and their perpetrators, the Nazis. The Germans "accepted" them neither more nor less than they had "accepted" scores of democratic governments in the post-war German Republic.

Attributing shrewd and complacent foresight to the German people with regard to what the Nazis were actually going to do is as fantastic as it is inhuman. The Germans expected the Nazis to fulfill the functions of government as every government in the post-war period had done or had attempted to do. This new party claimed it had a miracle cure for the blighting plague of unemployment. The Germans did not believe in it wholeheartedly; but their need for hope made them hope, at least half-heartedly. And as I heard many of them say, what harm could there be in letting "them" try, in letting them get used to working for the "common good?" God knows, the Nazis were past-masters in the art of cloaking their revolting misdeeds in the noble garb of the common good. But who knew it at that time?

When they enacted an innocent-looking regulation, "temporarily," as they put it, abrogating civil and political liberties, making all political activity save that of the Nazis illegal, they announced that this regulation was imperative for the common good and necessary to forestall any possibility of a Communist-Socialist uprising. At that time—in early 1933—when no one was even thinking of war, the mere thought of that other great curse of humanity called revolution, assured a comparatively positive response to such a "temporary" measure, since there was no immediate general objection to depriving revolutionaries of their means of fostering revolution through political agitation.

Again, when the vicious "liquidation" of former political adversaries began, that is, when the Nazis hit upon the simple device of throwing dissenters into concentration camps, they did so using the same label of "temporary measures necessitated by the common good and applied to a small number of politicians."

To understand the reaction of the Germans or, if

one prefers, their lack of reaction to these initial measures, to understand it in a spirit of unbiased objectivity, one must consider also the synchronization of the press (which occurred with less rapidity than that of the radio which had been state-controlled ever since its inception) and of the rigid control exerted in the selection and distribution of news. The Germans knew practically nothing of what was happening outside Germany and very little of what was going on in their own country. If and when they were confronted with monstrous stories which came to them by word of mouth, this people, as law-and-order-conscious as any people in the world, simply refused to believe them.

Even though human incredulity in the face of "unheard-of" happenings is a fairly well-known, normal phenomenon, the Germans, along with other normal traits (weaknesses as well as virtues), are often denied the "privilege" of this one too. "They must have known," goes the argument, for it is necessary that they should have believed what even the much better informed public abroad listened to with doubting ears, since otherwise it might become possible to sympathize with them and to understand their reaction. Well, by vice or virtue, they did refuse to believe what little they heard about the Nazi crimes. I can illustrate my point no better than by relating the following truly typical experience:

Shortly after the Nazis had come to power, the father of my girl friend whom I had known since my days at the university was arrested by the Nazis. He was a member of the *Reichstag* and had played a considerable role in the post-war politics of his *Land*. Being Jewish and a prominent member of the Socialist party, being honest, courageous, and true to his convictions, he had been the favorite object of hatred of the Nazi scum of his community. And now, there he was, locked up in one of the first concentration camps.

At this early date of the Nazi reign, the procedure was called *Schutzhaft*, protective custody. And actually, there was something more than devilish irony in this euphemistic designation, considering the gangs of youngsters propagandistically driven out of whatever little wits they had had, or the howling mob of hopeless, rootless, and ruthless political rowdies in Nazi garb roaming the streets in starry-eyed paroxysm of national sentiment and shouting the threats of their battle-songs.

My own people and others who learned about the arrest of my friend's father said: "Thank God! At least 'they' cannot lay hands on the men in *Schutzhaft*. Once the storm blows over, they will be released or there will be a trial and everything will be all right." My friend's father himself was firmly convinced that such lawless acts would soon be righted and that he would be free to resume his life with his family.

At the end of a year he was murdered, strangled by two notoriously shady characters with police records.

Political murder! One felt that something had to happen. Yet nothing did happen. The few who knew about it met with the absolute refusal on the part of friends and acquaintances to believe that such a vile thing had happened in Germany. Surely, such things could occur in far-away Turkey or Siberia but not in Germany. "It just can't happen here!" People preferred to let themselves be convinced by the official version of suicide.

I then realized how the Nazis could actually get away with murder. The fantastic character and the reckless boldness of their crimes reaped them the benefit of decent people's refusal to believe the unbelievable. This could not be. My own parents refused to believe that this man had been murdered.

Those who came close to early Nazi crimes were few, very few. And life was going on.

At this moment the bulk of the German population was experiencing the comforting sensation of being relieved of active concern with politics.

They had had enough of party bickerings and political campaigns. Their general distrust of politicians, especially of the extreme left, was no less acute than it is in this country where the fact, for instance, that partisans of Communism are excluded from the Civil Service is rarely objected to, except perhaps by an occasional liberal or so-called progressive, or again by a few renowned lawyers like Arthur Garfield Hays and once in a while by certain newspapers and periodicals.

After the "temporary" abrogation of civil and political liberties, all the Arthur Garfield Hayses as well as newspapers and periodicals of pronounced liberal inclinations were forced into silence by threats of sterner measures. Again, of course, in the name of the common interest.

It must also be remembered that German dislike and fear of Communism was by no means artificially engendered by such methods as the *Reichstag*-fire fake. Scores of people—even though by no means the entire population—did know that the *Reichstag* fire was a Nazi vote-getting trick, a kind of shock treatment to obtain an electoral majority. But their and their fellow-countrymen's fear of Communism was real, *Reichstag* fire or not. The basis of it was the behavior of Communist politicians and their followers throughout the post-war period. One must have little understanding of

Western civilization to be surprised at the lack of regret on the part of the Germans to see the wire-pullers of that lopsided and delusive political theory reduced to silence and inaction. Had they not given abundant proof that they were nothing but a bunch of irresponsible politicians who had done their utmost to make all attempts at parliamentary democracy in post-war Germany an unworkable joke?

But of all these points the most important one to bear in mind is that all the initial so-called "temporary" measures were imposed upon people utterly weary of political strife and exhausted by material misery. This of course made it easier for the Nazis to inject their insidious venom slowly and in a way that kept the real meaning of their measures away from the people. The building up of the Gestapo, for instance, to that formidable, all-engulfing organization, a veritable strait jacket for the Germans up to the day of the Nazis' final defeat, did not occur in one day. It too was disguised under the noble colors of the common interest and the prevention of revolution.

Not even the initial measures against the Jews seemed to portend any of the horrors of the treatment they were to receive in later years. A fact that cannot be stressed too much is that the overwhelming majority of the German Jews themselves were far from being unusually alarmed until it was too late. Their reactions and attitudes were in no sense different from those of their "Aryan" fellow-countrymen. Many German Jewish refugees in this country have lost all sense of proportion in their understandable though tragic hatred against the entire nation some members of which became guilty of the most heinous crimes against the Jewish people, but few, if any, of these refugees will be bold enough to assert that they foresaw what was coming and were possessed of greater perspicacity than the rest of the Germans.

It is also to be noted that right at the beginning there were not a few Germans who did not feel that it was particularly unjust that the admission of Jews to certain professions should be kept in proportion to their representation in the population as a whole. Constituting, as they did, one per cent of the population of the country, some people did not find it unjust that the number of Jewish doctors, lawyers, students, etc., should not be allowed to surpass one per cent of the total corps of German doctors, lawyers, students, etc. I am of course speaking of the very initial measures, which indeed did not differ so very much from the quota system applied, I am told, by quite a number of American universities with rather uncompromising strictness. I do not allude to this parallel to whitewash the German people's lack of concern about certain measures which, at the outset, did not seem particularly vicious and which became catastrophes only much later when any reference to the responsibility of the German people had lost all meaning.

Neither in this nor in any other respect am I interested in "whitewashing" my people. I merely want to show that neither their foibles nor their strengths differentiate them strikingly from any other people on this globe. At any rate, the nation that would have a right to look down upon the Germans and despise or condemn them for this or that valid reason, remains to be created.

But to come back to the question of the initial measures against the Jews. The one-per-cent quota was filled by veterans who remained in their government or civilian jobs. And of course, all this was presented to the population as "temporary measures" which the German people considered unfortunate concessions on the part of the government to certain fanatic supporters but which they were convinced would soon be dropped again. And while we are on the subject let me state —and why should it not be stated?—that I knew a considerable number of Jews who would have been very willing supporters of the Nazi form of government, had it not been for the handicap of their race which not even Goebbels proved smart enough to remove by discovering of a sudden that some Jews were Aryans.

Another measure which was taken and which made for encouragement rather than discouragement under this new government was the expansion of labor service. It was neither said nor believed to be a camouflaged form of military service. The German people actually welcomed it as a means of taking their miserable, hopeless, and jobless youths off the streets and out of barrooms and of putting them to work that would prove useful to themselves and the community.

When, a little later, the Nazi government entered upon its vast program of public works—the miracle cure for unemployment they had been trumpeting about — do you suppose they announced to the German people that the highways to be built would be roads of strategic importance? Scarcely. What they did announce was that these fine roads were to be used by every German who, thanks to the government's marvelous management of public affairs, would soon drive his own car. In all fairness to the German people, let me add that they took this propaganda boast with more than a grain of salt. But Germans are human beings, just like everyone else. And glittering promises, following the misery they had endured during the entire post-war period, induced in them a very human readiness, or indeed, eagerness to believe in miracles.

As a matter of fact, the effect of the Nazi New Deal was the immediate absorption of large numbers of unemployed. The people in no way realized that what it actually amounted to was merely an ever-increasing accumulation of public debts. What they saw was the disappearance of the curse of unemployment. But the Nazis reaped an immense political harvest out of this success; for those who visualized the dangers of such a policy were very few, and the same would have held true for any other country as well.

Pretty soon, however, it became obvious that the Nazis were passionately interested in things other than the betterment of German living conditions and a rational management of public affairs in the common interest. Only a few months after their rise to power they set out upon the realization of their program to do away with the "injustices of the Treaty of Versailles."

Their first step in this direction was to quit the scene of Geneva, the League of Nations. This sudden turn to "foreign policy," which now became the Nazis' chief concern, one to which everything else was to be subordinated, had the same effect on the Germans that it would have had on any other people in the world, that of uniting them.

Whoever feels inclined to jump at conclusions as to the wickedness of the Germans on the ground of their lack of violent reaction against the Nazi regime and its foreign policy, whoever reproaches the Germans for having "tolerated" this government, wantonly disregards two socially important and essential facts: The first is the strong sentiment for the common interest which is innate in the Germans. It became highly developed because of the hardships they had endured, for trouble and misery have a way of making people huddle together for mutual comfort and consolation. The other fact, which is too often forgotten by judges of German iniquity, is the German people's highly developed sense of justice and equity, not—to be sure—a distinctively German trait but rather one of the finest fruits of civilization and in turn proof of the high level attained by any nation possessed of it.

The most complete disregard for, or utter ignorance of, the fact that the German sentiment of justice and equity is at least as strong as that of any other civilized people, characterizes the attempts made within the past few years, notably by refugee writers, to represent the Germans as backward barbarians in a civilized world. Whether the thesis is based on wanton lies or on revolting ignorance is less important than the fact that it has been widely disseminated among people who have no way of getting acquainted with the German people except through the falsehoods they read. This makes a reasonable approach to the "German problem" still more difficult.

But we must not pursue this inexhaustible topic beyond the point necessary to bear out our contention that it is by no means surprising that a good many Germans welcomed the Nazis' announcement that they were now ready to embark upon the realization of that part of their program which was designed to do away with the "injustices of the Treaty of Versailles." In concentrating on what they called foreign policy, they succeeded in killing several birds with one stone: they "proved" again that everything they did was done to serve the "common interest"; they concealed their amateurish fumbling with the great economic problems of the nation by subordinating them entirely to the great foreign problems; they justified their ignominious misdeeds with the famous label of "temporary" and "for the prevention of the rebirth of internal political strife" and proclaimed as their goal an equal voice for Germany in the international concert; they solved the problem of getting a firm grip on the nation by playing on the people's sentiment of justice, thereby stirring up their passions; they claimed to have found the only cure to all the evils of our modern times in the fiery idealism for a common cause which they succeeded in evoking in their followers. Their entire activity cannot be described better than by calling it the rape of a civilized people by a gang of public-welfare hoodlums whose infamous political maneuverings were thoroughly un-German.

Little heed is given to such obvious evaluations by the prosecution. Mankind's experience is cavalierly cast to the winds in order to obtain one or more of a variety of momentary goals. The cunning devil which appears through the backdoor of all our splendid individual heritage of Western civilization is treated by the prosecution with oblivion; and yet it was that cunning devil, riding on racial, religious, economic, and national prejudices, on accumulated resentment and on the mass of running sores in man's social-political life which was being released on the Germans with a propagandistic genius and a religious fervor which it would have taken any people more than human forces to withstand.

Those of us who have ever so slight a notion of psychology, even if it be based exclusively on self-observation, know that men obey their instincts,

sentiments, and desires far more readily than rea-
soned reflection. When we judge someone else's
actions and reactions, we usually voice merely the
sentiments which his behavior evokes. We seldom
take the trouble of giving the case further thought.
The same applies when the "someone else" is not
just an individual but a foreign people involved in a
certain situation. Here, too, we allow ourselves to
judge quite humanly as our sentiments and instincts
dictate. But in doing this, whether we are indulging
in admiration or condemnation, we very frequently
make a grave mistake: we base our judgment on
conditions existing for us whereas those we are
judging may be acting on the basis of completely
different premises.

When people in this country reproach the Germans for having "tolerated" the treatment inflicted
upon the Jews by the Nazis, they set out—naturally but wrongly—from concepts which pre-
vail in their own environment. The very essence
of these concepts is to consider the Jews as different only in so far as they belong to a different religious creed. On that basis, any attempt to submit
them to a discriminatory treatment must seem revolting; and the idea of persecution must revive
the terror with which mankind was haunted during the days when religious fanaticism was rampant.

However, what was done to the Jews in Germany was conceived, publicized, and executed in the name of the common interest, not against the members of a different religious creed but as measures of protection against the members of a different and supposedly highly dangerous race. For those who have swallowed the myth of the viciousness of the Prussian race without bothering to verify it, it should not be impossible to understand that a part of the German people became victims of the myth of the wickedness of the Jewish race. It should be as possible to understand this as it is to understand the concept differentiating between Negroes and Whites in this country.

Furthermore, in connection with the Jewish question it should be stated that the superficial interest most people take in foreign peoples and their lack of factual information about them, make many of them prone to lose completely any sense of comparative values. Being ashamed of or revolted at the Nazi politicians' revival of practices which we had thought of as belonging to the deep dark past, we easily forget not only that the enactment and execution of measures against the Jews took place gradually, but we forget that 83 per cent of the German voters (17% being Communists) were interested primarily in measures for the prevention of revolution. Measures against the leaders and the rank and file of a political party openly advocating and propagating a Communist revolution overshadowed by far and very naturally the fate of one per cent of the population of the country.

Moreover, the predominant role played by Jews in the basic program and intellectual leadership of Communism can also reasonably be supposed to have influenced many Germans to feel that those fellows (vaguely identifying Communists and Jews after the less naïve and innocent model of the Nazi demagogues) were finally getting what they had coming to them.

When one reads or hears about the Germans under the Nazis, one generally gets a very quick résumé of all the appalling crimes of the Nazi regime and its tools against the very essence of civilization. The reaction of disgust and revolt is so instantaneous and so sure that one forgets or does not take the time to realize that the Germans never got a résumé of this kind. In Germany things happened slowly. Most measures were termed tentative and were actually believed to be temporary. They were explained and justified as imperative in the common interest by a propaganda as skilful as it was diabolical.

The Germans were deprived of all the news save what Goebbels handed out gratis, and millions of Germans are learning only today what went on in their country after the Nazis' rise to power. The hundreds of thousands of German victims of the Nazi regime and the formidable terror organization of the party with its SS and its Gestapo are overwhelming proof of the fact that the Germans were terrorized to an almost inconceivable degree; yet in spite of all that, thousands and thousands did revolt and did pay dearly for their heroism.

However, the man in the street—in all countries and unfortunately or fortunately in Germany too— is neither interested in heroism nor inclined to look at things philosophically "under the aspect of eternity." He has no time to do more than take care of himself, his job, and his family. He wants to work and enjoy the fruits of his labor and feels content when he can be convinced—rightly or wrongly— that the men in Washington, Berlin, Paris, or London are qualified to take care of the rest. How natural, then, that the Nazis should have found support and even approval among the millions of unemployed men and women who, thanks to this new regime, were able to find jobs.

Was it really criminal on their part not to feel an urgent desire to rebel against their "benefactors" because of the treatment applied to an infinitesimal portion of the population? Was it not normal and human that the possibility of losing their jobs outweighed the desire of innumerable civil servants to demonstrate against the regime? If one looks at it in this light, who is still ready to cast the first stone? The best among us who are pure in heart and heroes in ideals and action, refuse to judge and condemn. Their broad humanity forbids them to do so.

Yet criticism remains rampant—of course from a safe distance in space and time. That the Germans should have "tolerated" their disgraceful regime can only be construed as a major crime against humanity if one accepts the views of these stone-throwers of whom a by no means negligible contingent is made up of German refugees. These people always tempt me to ask why they did not stay in Germany and rebel, or why they did not return there for that purpose. They were deprived of their political rights? So were the Germans. The Gestapo was pursuing them? The Gestapo was pursuing every German who dared utter a word of disapproval against the regime. They were prohibited by law from forming groups which could organize a nucleus of revolt and resistance against the regime? So were the Germans. They were considered pariahs in Germany? So were all the Germans who were known to have been or to be adversaries of the Nazis.

When, in June, 1934, a number of Nazi public-welfare playboys, together with some former political foes, were murdered, it dawned upon the

German people that the very essence of the activity of the Nazis was the establishment of ruthless domination and unlimited dictatorship for the sake of mad "political ideas." But who really cared about Nazis being killed? On the contrary, the more of them were murdered, the fewer remained and the better it was. Who realized that the decree by which Hitler "justified" these murders some days after the event and by which he appointed himself "Supreme Law Lord of the Nation," signified actually the establishment over the Germans of a regime of lawlessness such as Europe had not known since the darkest days of the dark ages? Few, very few, in Germany as well as abroad; and the German residents among those few could speak about it only at the risk of Dachau or Buchenwald.

There is little doubt but what Hitler's madness of June, 1934, will remain the outstanding feature of his reign of terror. But while it was happening, everyone was being submitted to a relentless flow of propaganda which hammered into the minds of the German people the refrain that all these events were unfortunate but inevitable, that all this was temporary, that Germany's public life would fall to pieces if political strife were permitted to become so much as a mere threat, that the shock treatment against the curse of unemployment would fail and upset the entire economic system if confidence in the stability of the government were even questioned, that the Nazi foreign-policy program permitted of no internal troubles, and so on and so forth. At that time the Nazi government had managed already to place the Germans in the strait jacket of party organization and new regulations incorporated in the legal system, so that any attempt to get rid of the regime had by now become suicide. One great hope remained—that the outside world would soon find a way of making it impossible for the Nazis to ride down every domestic obstacle on the miracle horse of success in foreign policy.

Whoever tries to look at the Germans under Nazi rule with the sincere purpose of ascertaining what actually happened to them must be struck by the amazing role which foreign policy played for the Nazi government. Only blindness could prevent anyone from seeing why these Nazi madmen and public-welfare amateurs made the Reich's foreign policy their foremost concern. Here they could prove, as they put it in the broadcasts to which they subjected the German people for twenty-four hours a day, that their sole purpose was to wipe out the "injustices of the Treaty of Versailles" and to regain a "status of equality for the Germans."

Some months after their rise to power, they banged the door at Geneva. It was at a time when the League of Nations had become, not only in the eyes of the Germans but of a number of other nations, far more a rostrum for grandiloquent politicians than an institution where rational action was prepared and taken in the interest of all the peoples of this earth.

What member of any nation represented by those grandiloquent politicians, what member of any nation whose politicians were in some other way responsible for the weakness of the League, can blame the Germans for having succumbed to the roaring of Nazi propaganda harping everlastingly on the fact that their misery during the post-war years was due to a situation which the political wire-pullers of the former Entente (*Feindbundmächte*) were trying to maintain by means of the vaudeville show of Geneva? And still less room for blame would seem to remain when one understands that the German troubles at the time—whatever their causes may have been—were certainly not due to either a lack of willingness on the part of the Germans to work or to their inadequate skill in coping with obstacles in the pursuit of those aims for which the common man the world over is living and striving.

Can one reproach the Germans with having applauded their government's action in quitting Geneva at a time when the whole world was becoming aware of the fact that in great political decisions on questions of general disarmament or prevention of war, on questions where the life and death of peoples were at stake, the Geneva procedure and ideology had proved to be a failure? Let me quote a few passages from the valedictory of the representative of Chile announcing, in 1938, the withdrawal of his country from the League. In retrospect these passages represent a stern review of the political activities pursued within the realm of the League's ideology ever since the peacemakers of 1919 endowed mankind with this child of their imagination. The diplomat in question said:

"We are the first to recognize that opinion amongst Member States is not uniformly at one with our appreciation of the position, although a statistical retrospect of the political activities of the League shows that with its present legal structure and as regards the application of coercive measures, the League has never been able to find solutions for any political dispute.

"Of the forty-two political disputes which have been dealt with by the League since it came into existence, eleven (related almost without exception to matters connected with the liquidation of the great war) were a subject of decision by the Council. The other thirty-one disputes have either been settled by direct negotiations between the parties, or have been referred to other international organizations, or have led to a note signifying withdrawal from the League of Nations, or have been abandoned or left in suspense.

"This balance-sheet of results is, in the opinion of Chile, sufficiently eloquent to make comment unnecessary. But I note that the cold eloquence of figures, cogent as it is, is not sufficiently cogent to shake the views which are held in favor of the maintenance of a juridical *status quo* which to my government appears to be fatal alike to peace and to good understanding between nations.

"It is not without deep emotion that my country draws the moral of these discussions. But a conviction firmly embedded in the mind of my government and of public opinion in my country makes it impossible for Chile to continue to belong to the League of Nations while articles of the Covenant which are unenforced and unenforceable continue to figure in theory as part of the political structure of the League as we know it."

Not for one moment did the Nazis relax in their preoccupation with foreign policy. Early in 1934 they concluded a pact of amity with the government of Poland.

Domestic difficulties, especially the "revolutionary" pressure of certain party moguls and their followers, and the unrest connected therewith, came to a climax with the bloody purge of 1934.

And scarcely had the Germans begun to realize the true character of the Nazi regime as reflected by these appalling events, when the propaganda drums of "justice" and the trumpets thundering against the "injustices of Versailles" began sounding again.

Without losing a minute, the Nazis began playing up the Saar question—the return of the German Saar to the Reich. It is well known that the date of the Saar plebiscite had been determined along with the conditions creating the Saar status after the first World War. The plebiscite would have taken place, had the Hermann Müller or Brüning cabinet or, indeed, any other of the numerous postwar German republican cabinets been in power. As it was, Hitler happened to be holding the reins of government when it took place. But *der Führer* and his party loudspeakers made a big affair of it. And in January, 1935, an overwhelming majority of the Germans of the Saar voted for the return of their country to the Reich. They would have done so in any event and under any circumstances. But it was child's play for Nazi propagandists to foist this result upon the German people as another great success of Nazi policy.

The intensity of their propaganda was due to the regime's need for showing tangible results in order to keep the Germans in line. They were desperately in need of diverting the attention of the German public from internal events, for the Germans had become suspicious of this regime. The prosecution sees in the result of the plebiscite a proof for the fact that the Nazis represented exactly what the Germans wanted and needed. In attempting to judge what had happened they look for the complicated, being unable to grasp the obvious. The people of the Saar were Germans. The Saar wanted to be a part of Germany, not *because* of the Nazis but *in spite* of them.

Encouraged by their initial successes and eager to retain their psychological grip on the German people, the Nazis continued to apply the "wonder-working" devices of their foreign policy and to feed the public fairy tales of the Nazi knight in armor saving Cinderella-Germany from the evil powers of the witchcraft of international politics, making a constant and skillful appeal to the Germans' passion for justice.

Thus, following an agreement between the French and British governments to abrogate disarmament, the Nazis decreed the reintroduction of military conscription in March, 1935. This meant of course the formal abolition of the military clauses of the Versailles treaty. What happened? Nothing. Was there any action from the outside in the wake of this decision? None whatever. The Nazi policy of banging doors having thus far succeeded, what argument was left to the German people against it and against the Nazi contention that military strength was a *conditio sine qua non* in foreign affairs?

In the eyes of the German people, the abrogation of disarmament on the part of the French and British governments was proof positive of the soundness of the Nazi methods of dealing with the former enemies. Nothing succeeds like success, and nothing fails like failure. Had not the Germans been given a wonderful object lesson of the crude truth of this old adage when they were witnesses to the fact that a timid and practically unarmed attempt of the republican German and Austrian governments to ease Austria's economic difficulties by means of an Austro-German customs union had roused a storm of protest, while the mere threat of the Nazis to rearm massively had induced foreign governments to open new parleys? Did they not watch the British government negotiating a naval agreement with the Nazi government and see these negotiations actually culminate in the agreement of June, 1935?

Another Nazi success which strengthened their hold on the German people, was the visit paid to Hitler by Anthony Eden and John Simon. One must be blind or incapable of visualizing the effect of such official demonstrations on the people involved, if one refuses to admit the tremendous importance of this official British visit to Hitler, the murderer of 1934! In the eyes of the Germans it took on the character of a blessing from Great Britain on the Nazi gang; it became a major trump in the Nazis' efforts to sell the Germans the idea that the method of banging doors and playing with firearms was perhaps not so bad after all. What better proof could one ask than the approval of highly respected Great Britain?

For years the Germans had been subjected to ruthless propaganda onslaughts by politicians whose attempts to get their votes were tuned to the magic words, "Injustices of Versailles," magic because the Germans possess that wonderful and dangerous seed of civilization which, as we have had occasion to remark, must be seen in man's passion for justice. The painstaking efforts of the German republican governments to relieve hardship and struggle had never been crowned with glittering success, whereas Nazi door-banging and unilateral abrogation of treaty clauses had brought high-ranking British officials to Berlin and had actually resulted in new agreements!

More astonished themselves perhaps than anyone else at the simplicity of living and thriving on foreign successes, the Nazis became more and more involved in foreign enterprise. They did not have to invent a program: it had been written by the peacemakers of 1919. What they had to do was merely to find a suitable technique of fomenting and fostering unrest so as to bring about certain events which then required their intervention in the "common interest" of all concerned. To this end they adopted the method which had been so brilliantly and effectively employed by Communism, that of not letting the right hand know what the left hand is doing . . .

In terms of politics this meant giving assurances of proper behavior as a government and, at the same time, having the "people" (the fanatics of Danzig, the Sudeten, and Austria, for instance), acting under orders of party chiefs, create unrest and thus prepare the big events. If this tricky game, this obvious swindle did not bother the British government, why should the German people have felt it necessary to get wrought up to the point of starting a revolution?

By this time—we are still in 1935—another of Europe's "have-nots," led by as boisterous a politician as Hitler, turned from domestic problems to "foreign policy." Il Duce's thirst for Empire—a colonial empire to be acquired not at the cost of France or Great Britain but at the cost of one of the few still independent "backward" peoples of Africa—led to events which made everyone understand that any attempt to maintain peace by enforcing the ideology of the peaceful League of Nations could only wind up in war. Even though jurists the world over would have called such a "league war" by the euphemistic term of "sanctions" applied to Italy, it would have been war. The clearest statement of the situation was voiced by Mr. Baldwin, then Prime Minister of Great Britain, when in taking a stand against military sanctions he said: "It would be the most appalling irony of history if the League of Nations succeeded solely in provoking a general world-conflagration."

Encouraged by the leniency shown towards the Italian venture, the Nazis were soon to take up the realization of another of their aims of foreign policy, the remilitarization of the Rhineland. On the basis of "sovereignty" and "equality" they used the Franco-Russian alliance of 1935 as a pretext for denouncing the Locarno Pact and for translating this denunciation into action by having a few troops march into the Rhineland and take up quarters there.

In spite or perhaps because of their craving for justice, the Germans viewed this step with mixed emotions, prompted by two considerations: first, this meant that peace was at stake; and second, this was an encroachment on what they felt was lawful and just. This time the Germans knew that the question was not one of doing away with some particular injustice imposed upon them by a peace treaty, or contesting an impossible economic situation created by such a treaty. This time they knew that the Nazis were attacking a treaty they had agreed to and which they considered in line with their aim of collaborating with the other European governments in the establishment of a new European *modus vivendi*. This time the Nazis could find no way of playing up the injustices of Versailles. They knew it as any clearsighted observer did.

No move was ever based more on probability than the march into the Rhineland. German commanders carried sealed orders to be opened in case of military reaction on the part of the French. These orders called for immediate withdrawal. Any unprejudiced observer knew that even a threat of reaction, had it been concrete, would have given the German people a fair chance of wringing the necks of their oppressors. But the fruits of the Italo-Ethiopian dealings had become ripe. Whereas in that unsavory affair it had been Monsieur Laval's privilege to step on the brakes for the sake of France's "Latin sister" in order to thwart any possibility of Britain's warships making themselves heard along the Mediterranean supply routes to Africa, it was now Mr. Eden who, during the sessions of the Council of the League of Nations at St. James, gave Monsieur Flandin to understand that in case of violent French reaction to the Nazi gamble, France must not count on British participation.

The only reaction that did come forth was a verbal condemnation of "Germany's" unilateral action. And the only effect that reaction could have was the one it did have: it furnished the Nazis propaganda material with which to polish their instruments of rape of the German people by playing up, in all safety, the "French will" to keep Germany down. Can one blame the German people for not having been more violent in their reaction than the British and French governments? They saw their hope of foreign reaction against Hitlerism and its ruthless methods go down the river, and they fell back upon the fervent hope that somehow it might still be possible to preserve peace after all.

The armament race then went into high gear everywhere. The Nazis had the tremendous advantage of being spared the trouble of having to account for their expenditures. They had the further advantage of being able to point to immediate benefits resulting from the second round of their New Deal. It absorbed all the unemployed and put them to work for the Nazi version of the "common good." Who wanted to revolt? And who could reasonably expect revolt in Germany because of a situation which had permitted the government to strengthen its position by riding the waves of its successes in foreign policy? . . .

But I need not pursue the march of events in the international field over the following years. The pattern was set, and the Nazis were careful not to deviate from it in any important respect. It has been my purpose to expose that pattern, not to pose as one more historian of a chain of occurrences which all of us remember. What matters is merely that nothing happened, nothing whatsoever that could have entailed a striking change in the situation of the German people whose fate continued to be at the mercy of a dictatorial regime geared to the whims of one man.

Wherever people live in organized social communities, there exists a natural gap between those who govern and those who are governed; between those who make the laws and administer justice and those who must abide by the laws or suffer punishment; between those who manage public affairs and those who undergo the consequences of good or bad management; between those who live on public funds and those who build them up by paying taxes; between those who make propaganda and campaign promises and those who fall for them; between those whose social functions put them in a place where they could do something about the maintenance of peace and those who can only hope that the efforts of the masters of the hour may succeed in avoiding the outbreak of a new attempt at suicide by the peoples of this world; between those who declare wars and those who have to fight them.

This gap between politicians and the people holds good for any people anywhere. It was an abyss in the case of the Nazi clique and the Germans living under their knout. And if I am asked to sum up in one concrete proof the long drawn-out argument I have had to present on this count, I would simply point to the regime of suppression, murder, and terror which the Nazis were obliged to set up over the German people in order to keep them in line. The Nazi overlords were forced to maintain their rule by the permanent and increasing use of "temporary" measures of terror—not because of the wickedness of an unfortunate people but because of the terrifying complication of the social apparatus which had fallen into their hands, but about whose adaptability to their own ends they could not be sanguine for a single moment.

6. The Role of International Law in World Politics

We have looked at the Germans faced with the Nazi struggle for power. We have shown their dismal plight under the Nazi heel. We have demonstrated the shallowness of the argument which the prosecution draws from history to "prove" the Germans' lust for war, to picture them as fiendish warmakers.

But still, there is the fact of this last war, the World War of 1939, the initial stages of which saw the German armies pouring all over Europe. Only twenty years after the end of the First World War, humanity again had to put up with the great scourge of war. Again people suffered and died for "justice," for "democracy," for "liberty," for "*la patrie*," or the "fatherland." And why did it have to happen? The prosecution's answer is confoundedly simple. It's the fault of the German people. It's the fault of the Germans, of every German. It's my fault, I presume.

In all this very little heed is paid to the need for a fair evaluation of the situation in which the German people found itself; and yet, no one can fail to see that more than any other civilized people, the Germans were deprived of even the smallest influence on the course of action taken by their government in international politics.

Not only people who are thoughtless enough to approach the complex business of international affairs with the simplifying idea of blaming a race or a class but fair-minded people too who join but half-heartedly in the prosecution's jubilant *vae victis*: those who know that it is a hazardous venture to give preference to one set of facts rather than to another in an attempt to determine the causes of war; all those who are inclined to attribute to President Roosevelt's torpedoing of the London Economic Conference in 1933 at least as much responsibility for the second World War as to Nazi shenanigans or overall German wickedness—all these will find little satisfaction in seeing the hypothetical villain "Germany" exonerated and therewith eliminated as the scapegoat on which to heap humanity's misgivings and their pent-up emotional urge for punishment.

The defense, too, is dissatisfied with merely shattering the prosecution's arguments. With the problems of war and peace on our hands and minds, it is not enough to have contributed to clearing a people from the abominable accusation of being solely responsible for the misery of millions. An effort must be made to explain how and why generations of civilized people could have been led around for centuries from wars to peace, from peace to wars. The magnitude and seriousness of the problem should no longer be hidden behind some short-sighted prosecutor's skill in fixing the blame on millions of vanquished individuals and in making us let it go at that.—The real culprit must be found!

The real culprit is not an individual; not any limited number of individuals; not seventy million vanquished Germans, forty million Frenchmen, forty-six million Englishmen, one hundred and forty million Americans, two hundred million Russians; the culprit is no more any number of individuals than any form of political regime; he is not any separate set of social, economic, or psychological factors. *The culprit is international law,* a number of fundamental fallacies which have been, over long centuries, and still are, at the basis of the foreign policies of all civilized peoples.

The real culprit is to be found in those incredibly fallacious concepts which have beset the mas-

ters of man's destiny over hundreds and hundreds
of years and have made all efforts toward peaceful coexistence of nations a mockery—concepts
which represent nothing short of dynamite as far
as peace is concerned; concepts which—even if
nothing but good will and a highly developed sense
of responsibility for the fate of mankind had guided
our statesmen—would nevertheless have brought
about the unholy international mess and disorder
that upset the economic systems of the world, en-
tailing misery everywhere and a consequent readiness on the part of the common man to succumb to
political alchemists; concepts which, since they
became the guiding principles in international
affairs and foreign relations, are at the very root
of what leads nations through that vicious circle
of wars and peace treaties, of peace treaties and
wars; concepts which, though capable of raising the
hopes of the world for peace by showing the shining side of "justice among nations," are hiding
a reverse enabling them to hurl nations against one
another and to fan their emotions into medieval
passion for, or sublime abandonment to, the cause
of justice; concepts which, instead of promoting
and expediting mutual understanding and intelligent cooperation among peoples, have proven over
and over and over again to be an unsurmountable
road-block; concepts which, instead of making us

look at war as an appalling *social disease,* make us consider it an "international crime," compel people to indulge in frantic absurdities as to the criminal character of whole peoples and lure us on to the field of non-existing things like those fictitious "great actors of history" such as "Germany," "France," the "United States," etc.; concepts which permit vicious oppressors of mankind to conceal their selfish aims under the noble colors of justice and to drag millions of innocent people into war, death, and destruction by camouflaging the path of hatred and personal ambition with fake palms and wreaths, and by launching "agreements" and bombastic declarations overhead where they float through space in the garb of doves of peace.

In order to get a clear picture of the fallacious character of the concepts of international law as a vehicle for policies of peace, we will glance at a recent chapter of history, close enough for us to remember and yet sufficiently distant for us to see it in its true perspective.

According to the traditional ideology concerning international politics and foreign affairs, the period of "peace" following the last war was governed by the peace treaties of 1919. The politicians of the victorious nations worked long and hard on the treaties before they called the German representatives to hear the verdict and sign it—unless they wished to expose their country to foreign military rule. They had deemed it essential to punish "Germany" as the "criminal" responsible for the war.

The termination of the first World War, the "peace" treaties and the activities of politicians in charge of the management of public affairs in their respective countries in the post-war period, were governed by concepts of international law. The idea of terminating a war and introducing the period of peace by a "treaty" is a concept of international law *par excellence*. According to the opinions of social scientists, and especially of jurists, peace treaties are considered the normal way of ending a war. The authors of the most universally recognized books on international law are unanimous in saying that it is "reasonable" that a treaty of peace should be the normal end of war. And indeed, if we take the trouble to glance back at a relatively short period of international history, say about three hundred years, we come across hundreds of peace treaties concluded for the purpose of establishing peace after war. But their very number should suffice to make us suspect that most of them served readily as a justification for preparing the next round of hostilities. We naturally begin to wonder whether this accepted way of blessing mankind with *treaties* of peace instead of achieving the *establishment* of peace really deserves to be called "reasonable."

In the case of the peace treaties at the end of the first World War, the really acting persons were the politicians who at that time happened to fulfill socially important functions in their respective countries. They, aided by their experts, worked out the treaty and affixed their signatures to it, but they acted as if they were representing someone else—the "victors" or the "vanquished"—mysterious absentees who apparently had given these politicians full power of attorney to act on their behalf.

We are accustomed to speak of "France" as a person, a beautiful woman called "Marianne"; or of the "United States" as upright and righteous "Uncle Sam"; or of "Germany" as poor, dumb, and, for a time, swastika-ridden "Michael"; or again of "Great Britain" as rich "John Bull" without nerves or with nerves of steel. In doing so we succumb to a habit of primitive man, a habit which springs from the tendency to humanize social and other, at first glance intangible, forces and phenomena because we do not succeed in understanding them otherwise.

Lacking time, interest, training, or the leisure to know or learn about the whole complex pattern of facts, we create in our minds a simple and pal-

pable something to act in their stead. We humanize
the various organized societies and then proceed
to look at them with the same eyes with which we
are wont to look at individuals; we apply to them
the same concepts which we have learned to apply
to individuals. The fact that today many social
scientists, especially jurists, are still indulging in
this primitive tendency is but imperfectly covered
up by their endeavor to give themselves some sort
of a "scientific" justification in admitting that such
personified entities, the peace treaty makers in
the background, are mere useful fictions, something along the lines of symbols in chemistry.

Being as subject as other mortals to the prevailing
concepts of society, peace, and international politics, the politicians back in 1919, instead of making
peace, elaborated and concluded a treaty between
personified social entities, that is, mentally human-
ized fictions. In the treaties themselves *they applied the concepts of law which govern relations
among individuals.*

The very essence of the whole peace treaty affair
was the distinction between vanquished and
victor. Translated into terms of individual relations,
this means the condemnation of the vanquished as
a basis for the penalty to be decreed in the verdict
of the victor. Because of our tendency to humanize
social phenomena, such a parallel of relations be-

tween organized peoples to those between individuals seems quite natural. Mr. Lloyd George—speaking in defense of the peace treaty job with specific reference to the question of "reparations" and the "taking away of territories"—stated in his *The Truth About the Peace Treaties*:

"But the question to pay compensation for damage done by a wrong-doer and the payment by a defeated suitor of the costs incurred in a vindication of justice are among the integral principles of Law in every civilized community. States are not immune from the application of that elementary doctrine of jurisprudence." And he continues: "As far as principles of right are concerned, States must abide by the same rules of justice which they impose upon their citizens."

In addition to the disturbing fact that the transposition to the international field of the rules of law as applied to individuals within organized communities, is based upon the most backward legal-social superstition which makes the various organized peoples appear to us as "entities" capable of "acting," of "breaking the law," of being "punished" and "held responsible for damage" or again of being able to "dispose of their rights and property (territory and economic resources) at their own volition without regard to the fate of humanity," the easy parallel between the relations among individuals and those among "states" (or nations or powers or acting persons of history) as governed by the same rules of law, suffers from this very serious fallacy:

If individuals clash over a question of contractual relations, they are not allowed to take the law into their own hands. They go before a judge who imposes the "rules of law" with the most powerful social machinery to back him up. If individuals do not abide by the verdict, various means are provided to make them do so. But when international disputes arise, and when these disputes touch upon "great political questions" such as territory, populations, foreign rule, interpretation of treaties, and the like, the only methods so far available to determine what is "right" have been discussions among politicians and their helpers (legal experts and diplomats). If such discussions lead to a peaceful solution, by one or both of the parties' giving in, everything is all right and there is no problem. But if one or both of the parties insist upon what *they* deem right or on *their* particular way of interpreting a treaty, the further development of the case depends upon the scope of the dispute, the possibilities a politician has of adopting an inflexible attitude with a chance of getting public support, the resources the parties have at their disposal, and their readiness to use such resources if necessary. In serious disputes of this kind, so-called international law offers *no method other than war* for determining who is "right." When one of the parties is vanquished, the victor is "right" and imposes the "law." *

Paltry and impotent jurists, blinded by age-old superstition and a complete inability to see things as they really are, try to calm their uneasiness at the obvious shortcomings of such a "law" by calling international law a law as yet incomplete, a law in an early stage of development, fit for improvement. None of these masters of legal superstition has ever given an inkling of proof that the mortal danger which these concepts represent for mankind in the hands of politicians is anything but the law of the jungle.

The most recent and the most widespread product of the minds of the majority of jurists and legally minded politicians is the idea of improving international law by endowing some international authority with sufficient means to "enforce the peace!" I need not enlarge at this point upon the appallingly false and ludicrously absurd idea of "enforcing peace." It is a contradiction in terms and switches any future chance of peace from the frying pan into the fire.

* I cannot refrain, at this juncture, from calling attention to the fact that international law is not a German invention.

But let us look briefly at what the management of international affairs by politicians basing their activities on international law was like during the last post-war period.

Once the Germans, at the point of exhaustion and encouraged by the lenient-sounding fourteen points of President Wilson, had laid down their arms, the victors elaborated the peace treaties, the "law" destined to govern future international relations. Instead of liquidating the war, instead of trying to eliminate its causes by starting a period of fruitful international collaboration on great economic and social problems, they linked the fate of mankind to a treaty which represented the law of the victors. They punished, exacted reparations, created the League of Nations as an international authority, and settled down to bend their efforts on maintaining the new order. It had always been done that way.

To have the "peacemakers" do anything else, would have presupposed a clear insight into the true character of the concepts of law, which within organized societies are prevented from becoming dangerous by the permanent pressure put upon individuals through a powerful legal mechanism. Such a mechanism being completely lacking in the international field, these concepts are here devoid of their necessary corollary. They are apt to provoke the most disastrous consequences because of their close association with the highly emotional habits of human beings, a fact which makes them such a favorite arsenal of innocent-looking weapons used by politicians to get their people where they want them.

Angered by innumerable criticisms leveled at the makers of the last peace treaties, Mr. Lloyd George defied all the critics and said that they ought "to measure the peace settlement by the highest standards of right attained in any civilized community" in order to discover that no one else would have been able to do a better job than he and his colleagues had done.

Indeed, when one accepts this parallel for the management of peaceful international coexistence, when one refuses to see that it represents a ghost-dance of fiction and false analogy and both the sowing of the seeds and the cultivation of the germs of the following war, then this is quite an argument. But those standards of right which, thanks to the elaborate legal mechanisms of the various communities, are the very conditions of peaceful coexistence of millions of individuals, are absolutely unfit as a guiding principle for the management of international affairs.

While the peacemakers were applying those standards of right, while they were quarreling about the degree of punishment to be inflicted upon "Germany" and the amount of reparations to be exacted from her because she was "responsible" for the damage done by the fact of the war, opinions were voiced which seem particularly pregnant in the light of what happened later on. Said Mr. Lloyd George in his famous Fontainebleau document:

"You may strip Germany of her colonies, reduce her armaments to a mere police force, and her navy to that of a fifth rate power; all the same in the end, if she feels she has been unjustly treated in the peace of 1919, she will find means of exacting retribution of her conquerors . . .

"The maintenance of peace will depend upon there being no causes of exasperation constantly stirring up the spirit of patriotism, of justice and fair play . . .

"We shall never make a lasting peace by attempting to restore the conditions of 1914 . . .

"If we are wise, we shall offer to Germany a peace which, while just, will be preferable for all sensible men to the alternative of Bolshevism . . .

"To my mind it is idle to endeavor to impose a permanent limitation of armaments upon Germany unless we are prepared similarly to impose a limitation upon ourselves . . .

"From every point of view therefore, it seems to

me that we ought to endeavor to draw up a peace settlement as if we were impartial arbiters, forgetful of the passions of war. This settlement ought to have three ends in view. First of all, it must do justice to the Allies by taking into account Germany's responsibilities for the origin of the war and for the way it was fought. Secondly, it must be a settlement which a responsible German government can sign in the belief that it can fulfil the obligations it incurs. Thirdly, it must be a settlement which will contain in itself no provocations for future wars, and which will constitute an alternative to Bolshevism, because it will commend itself to all reasonable opinion as a fair settlement of the European problems." (*The Truth About the Peace Treaties*, page 405.)

The first paragraph of this quotation would seem to show that at least one of the peacemakers of 1919 clearly predicted the course of future events. So much the more urgent is the question: How was it possible that all this happened? Why did it have to happen?

If one tries to find a "scientific" answer to these questions, that is, if one does some research in books and documents, one is bound to run across the opinion of scores of historians and social scientists who lay the blame on the leniency of the treaty makers toward "Germany," and of about an equal number of others who believe that the treatymakers should have been more severe. One will find books blaming Lloyd George for having been too friendly towards the Germans and others blaming Clemenceau for having allowed his passion for eating Germans to interfere with the dictates of common sense. One will have to listen to lengthy explanations by men who were themselves among the actors on the peace stage and who swear in their memoirs that they tried their very best to make a lasting peace. One will find authors who picture President Wilson as the dupe of hateful, vindictive, and rapacious European politicians and others who depict these same European politicians as the converts of an "American saint." But one will find scarcely anyone who bravely lays bare the roots of the evil, and who discovers that what happened in the past (and is happening again today) was bound to happen, could not have failed to happen because of the fundamentally wrong and disastrous notion that the rules of law governing the relations between individuals can be applied in the same way to the relations between States.

There is no doubt but what the political and economic consequences imposed upon the Germans by the peace treaties were the spontaneous expression of the highest standards of right ever reached in any civilized community. But in the international field, the application of the legal principles of "punishment" and "reparation" cannot be likened to the verdict of an impartial judge settling disputes among individuals because there is no powerful impartial judge who applies the rules of law, but the powerful victorious party which tries to impose upon the vanquished what it—the victor—decrees to be just.

As to the disastrous consequences which the "application of international law" in the peace treaties of 1919 had for all humanity, let me quote two men widely known for their high intellectual standards whom no one can seriously suspect of having placed their faculties in the service of German propaganda or Prussian war-mindedness.

Said the late Professor Gustav Cassel, one of the few outstanding economists of our time: "In the post-war reconstruction period German reparations and other war debts stand out as disturbances of the first order." And Mr. Paul van Zeeland, former Belgian Premier and at one time chosen by the British and French governments to study the possibilities of international collaboration in economic and financial questions: "The treaties of peace in 1919 chose in some points solutions which ignored economics. The anti-economic seeds, incautiously scattered at that time, have sprouted; favored in their growth by the inevitable consequences of the war and by the mistakes (which were not inevitable) of post-war politics, they have borne the poisonous fruit from which we are all suffering now." Such were the results of the disastrous, albeit sincere, endeavor of politicians to use the rules of international law as a means to establish peace.

But there is yet another point which may serve to illustrate the fact that any application of those rules of law after the fashion of the last peace treaties is worse than a crime against the fate of humanity; that it is a hair-raising stupidity committed by politicians who are slaves to traditional thinking, who sacrifice to a momentary satisfaction of the sentiments of "justice" all rational attempts to prevent mankind from continuing to waste its forces, its ingenuity, and the fruits of its labor on futile efforts to gain illusory advantages by the destruction or enslavement of select nations and peoples, and—worst of all—who nonetheless pay lip-service to the truth that the well-being of all civilized peoples can result only from intelligent cooperation between governments on real problems, and not from sterile bickerings over agreements, treaties, and other legal fineries.

The point I wish to stress concerns the special fallacy of the enlightened protagonists of "international law" according to whom the "legal persons" affected by international statutes are admittedly not real individuals but convenient symbols or fictions. This view implies that for instance "Germany" was "punished" according to "international law" and not the Germans. Now, this would be fine and lovely, for who cares if "Germany" is punished and suffers—or "France" or "Russia" or "Italy"—as long as we are assured that "Germany"—or "France" or "Russia" or "Italy" —are abstract fictions or symbols not to be identified with the concrete individual Germans—or Frenchmen, Russians, and Italians. The trouble is that when the fiction "Germany" was punished, millions of individual Germans had to suffer unspeakable misery as a consequence.

Why? Just what was the crime they had committed? That they had fought in the war? That they had fought for their country and had done their duty? It wasn't they who had declared war back in 1914. *That* the imperial German government had done, whereupon they merely did what every honest man the world over is expected to do when war "breaks out." They abided by the laws of their country. *Not doing so*, draft-dodging or desertion, *would have been a crime*. Can one expect any normal human being to accept being considered a criminal for having done his duty? . . . to accept being considered a criminal not by an impartial judge but by the victors? Can one wonder that a goodly percentage of those "criminals" responded to the relentless propaganda onslaught of politicians of the Nazi breed who promised to put an end to such injustice? One can wonder only that the response was not more general.

Or take the case of all the Germans who were born during the last war or shortly before and after. It was their generation in particular which was to succumb to Nazi propaganda riding the Trojan horse of justice. How could all those youngsters be expected to look forward to an uncertain future, to hopelessness and unending difficulties and tell themselves: All is well, right, and just: "Germany" was guilty, and we must suffer the consequences.— They saw no connection between their fate and the fact that they were supposed to go on enduring misery and hopelessness as "punishment" for a "crime" they could not possibly have committed. No wonder that a goodly number of them listened to those voices that told them that since they had committed no crime other than that of having been born in Germany, their desperate situation was the consequence of an injustice committed by foreign governments. *What is surprising* is rather the fact that so many of them resisted the voice of the Tempter and recognized the vile vanity of his promise.

But I have not finished yet with my theme song that what happened and goes on happening to the world is much less a consequence of the existence of the battered and mistreated German people than it is the inevitable result of the application of the concepts of international law to the management of international affairs.

Whereas up to the time of the first World War—in accordance with the traditional belief of peoples, politicians, rulers, historians, and legal and other "experts" on foreign policy—the "States" or "Nations" or "Powers" were "applying international law" to "international relations"; whereas it was these "great acting persons of history" who were "abiding by international law," who were reproaching each other with "breaking" or trying to break international law (treaties, for the most part), who were resorting to war as a legally sanctioned means of foreign policy (a means for which this same "international law" was endowed with innumerable rules and regulations); whereas it was they who were resorting to war in cases of "violation of their sovereign rights" (especially when there were fair chances of winning); whereas it was they who were concluding peace treaties and maintaining military and naval might in order to be able to defend their "rights": once the first World War was over, something new was added to the collection of legal concepts, something that had not existed in the peace treaties of the past. A new sprout of juridical fancy was grafted onto the old tree of "international law" and it was named by the name of the "League of Nations."

In addition to the ancient superstition according to which a peace treaty, that is, the imposition of the "law" of the victor upon the vanquished, is identified with "peace" and as such is signed by both victor and vanquished, certain additional "obligations" with respect to the maintenance of "justice" and the scrupulous respect for all treaty engagements were signed.

Today practically no one denies that the "creation" of the League of Nations exhausted itself in the compilation of a high-sounding supplement to the conventional legal vocabulary, inspired, perhaps, by the honest though fallacious desire on the part of individual politicians to do something more than politicians had formerly been expected to do after the termination of an armed conflict between sovereign powers. The League of Nations was an attempt to impart stability and permanence in terms of international law to a situation fixed by virtue of the power of the victors.

The novelty of it all did not consist in the fundamental purpose of the Covenant to serve as an instrument in the hands of the victors to maintain a situation brought about by the fact of their having been victorious but merely in that a new brand of legalistic fog was mixed in with the old brew to permit the pretense, at least for the time being, that international politics was to be handed over to an "international authority." Barring these legal niceties, however, the real actors of the League remained the self-centered politicians of the victorious "powers." The League simply *could* not do anything without "France" and "Great Britain"; and the small nations, admitted to membership with an "equal" voice, *would* not do anything without "Britain" and "France." These two, for better or for worse, were the masters of the League of Nations.

It was soon to become apparent that the Covenant was actually just another international political treaty. However noble and sincere its original aims, it soon became apparent that its effect was principally to warp the outlook of the politicians of the nations frequently assembled at Geneva; in no time they were again hopelessly entangled in curlicues of legal superstition, quarreling about "rights" and "obligations" of "states" instead of promoting international cooperation for the establishment of peace to which, to be sure, they continued to refer in empty verbiage or tragic self-deception as their most glorious goal.

A look at the records and minutes of both the Assembly and the Council of the League is revealing. One immediately becomes aware of the fact that the political debates at Geneva centered predominantly around legal concepts. One reads interminable discussions on "treaty obligations," their "interpretation and meaning," and the "rights" of the nations. One sees with stupefaction that the activity of politicians to whom millions and millions of plain people had entrusted their hopes for peace and decent living exhausted itself in debates closely resembling medieval debates of learned men on the question of how many angels can dance on a pin point or whether a camel could pass through a needle's eye.

The absence of an impartial authority prevented the League from resembling even remotely a functioning legal mechanism of international scope and resulted in all those wonderful debates which represent a perfect bonanza for a sarcastic Ripley of political inclinations. Here is a typical example of what I have in mind, and I swear by the beards of my ancestors that I am not trying to be funny but am simply citing some facts which are a matter of record and can be checked by anyone who cares to do so.

The Covenant provided for a strict limitation of the "right" of sovereign powers to resort to war and declared any war or threat of war a matter of concern to the entire League. When, in August 1923, Italian airplanes and ground forces bombed and occupied the Greek island of Corfu in reprisal for the murder of an Italian General and two officers of his suite supposedly by Greek patriots, the grave problem arose for the masters of the world assembled at Geneva as to whether or not it was the purpose of the League to restrict "compulsive measures" taken by one sovereign state to settle its differences with another. The statesmen composing the Council of the League were at a loss. By a resolution of September 28, 1923, they instructed a special commission of jurists to reply to certain questions raised in connection with the incident and regarding the interpretation of the Covenant. Here is number four of the list:

"Are measures of coercion which are not meant to constitute acts of war consistent with the terms of Articles 12-15 of the Covenant when they are taken by one member of the League without prior recourse to the procedure laid down in those articles?"

The legal master-minds replied that "coercive measures which are not intended to constitute acts of war may or may not be consistent with the provisions of Articles 12-15 of the Covenant, and it is for the Council, when the dispute has been submitted to it, to decide immediately having due regard to all circumstances of the case and to the nature of the measures adopted, whether it should recommend the maintenance or withdrawal of such measures."

After due discussion, the Council expressed high satisfaction with the perspicacious work of the jurists and approved their answer which in plain English signified that a spade is a spade except in cases where it is expedient to consider it a teaspoon.

It is not my purpose to turn legal-minded politicians of the post-war period to ridicule. I merely want to point out to what extent the minds of these politicians were befuddled by the ideology of international law which prevented them from turning their attention to the real problems in the fields of economics and finance. If we continue to believe in international law as a possible means for establishing peace, there can never be a peace which is more than an armistice and which will not inevitably lead to another war. Through the discussions of the League, one thing has become obvious: as long as concepts of "international law" involving "rights," "obligations," and "sovereignty" govern the activity of politicians, situations will always arise in which one of the parties insists upon its "rights" and has recourse to threats and, finally, to war. *For the very climax of the possibilities of international law in settling disputes is war.*

If the peace-killing potency of political treaties is in need of still further substantiation, nothing indeed could serve that purpose better than a reference to the amazing number of political treaties which the politicians in power concluded during the last post-war period in their endeavor to "maintain peace." If such political treaties between "the acting persons of history," treaties creating "rights and obligations" for those fictions, if this entire treaty business which is the very expression of the concept of international law were an appropriate means for bringing about or even for facilitating the peaceful coexistence of organized peoples, this second World War could not have been.

Indeed, during the last post-war period, the activity of the foreign service of all the various nations, of the ministers and diplomats as well as their inevitable companions, the legal experts, was by no means limited to the Sisyphean labors at Geneva. From the time of the peace treaties of 1919 to January, 1936, the men concerned with the conduct of foreign policy concluded one hundred and seventy "political treaties" of non-aggression, mutual assistance, friendship, guarantee, etc. In addition, one hundred and thirty political treaties concerned with the pacific settlement of disputes, treaties of investigation, arbitration, and conciliation were concluded during this same period. And this total of three hundred political treaties did not prevent the outbreak of a new World War. One might actually feel tempted to suspect that they not only failed to prevent it but in fact contributed greatly to bringing it about.

The Nazis did not neglect to take advantage of this traditional instrument of foreign policy. After winning their victory over the German people through falsehood, deceit, and crime, which put them in a position of power permitting them to take matters of foreign policy into their own bloody hands, political treaties were not just raining but fairly pouring over the world and especially over Europe.

Any keen observer knew that these rapidly concluded political treaties were proof of an impending storm. There was the German-Polish pact of amity. There was the German-British naval agreement. There was the minorities agreement between Germany and Czechoslovakia. There was the Munich pact, the German-French and the German-British friendship declarations, the neutrality guarantees for the benefit of the Netherlands, Belgium, and Denmark, the German-Russian non-aggression pact, and so on and so forth.

At the end of this came war, made a reality by the traditional last act of "peaceful foreign policy" —the declaration of war . . . No, it seems impossible to me—and it must seem so to anyone capable of looking at things without prejudice, that is, of visualizing in retrospect the busyness of politicians in charge of foreign policy, of picturing their frantic preoccupation with existing political treaties and their equally frantic concern with the conclusion of new ones, of recalling their worship of peace inside the temple of Geneva and their asseverations to their respective peoples that peace in justice and equality was their goal—it must seem impossible not to suspect a causal relationship between all that ado on the part of politicians and the outbreak of the second World War.

In spite of all this some people will still fall back on the easy escape from thought which consists in laying the blame on the Germans. I can hear their words—if there were no Germans, there would not have been a war. And of course, they are right. If there were no Germans, there could not have been a war between Germany and the Big Three, Four, Five, Six, Seven and their followers. Exactly as there could not have been such a war, if there were no Poles, Britons, Frenchmen, Americans, etc. It is a senseless type of reasoning that does not get you anywhere. In its essence it differs not a whit from the reasoning which time and again I have heard the hideous Nazis promulgate: If there were no Jews, this war would not have been.—You might as well argue: If men were angels, life on earth would be heavenly; if there were no humanity, there would be no problems—for us at least.

It is a merry-go-round method of proving things. The prosecution is very fond of it, for due to the general ignorance regarding the real nature of "international law," large sections of the public fail to see anything wrong in the argument that the Germans must be blamed for this war because "Germany" started it. And why did Germany start it? Because the German is a wicked, uncivilized, subhuman anthropoid, always waiting for *der Tag* when he can unleash the dogs of war and set them at an innocent world. War being the only state of things suited to the German way of life, the German barbarians wanted this war. They wanted it and should be blamed for it. Q. E. D.

At best the appalling fate of hundreds of thousands of German victims of Nazism will induce the prosecution to leave the door half-open for a strategic retreat into the senseless admission that there is a small percentage of "good Germans" who are the exception and therefore prove the rule that the overwhelming majority are thoroughly wicked.

It is, however, a simple fact that the Germans did

not want this war, that they dreaded it as all civilized beings dread war. To provide proof for this contention—a sounder and more convincing proof than the prosecution can ever hope to adduce for its shaky sophistry—one need only point to the fact that the Nazi government never ceased promising peace to the Germans. Why should they have done so if the people wanted war? They promised peace in honor and justice, a peace which would put an end to the discriminatory treatment which characterized the last post-war period when the Germans were generally considered a *quantité négligeable*.

The Nazis preached to the Germans what politicians the world over preached to their respective peoples: that peace, nothing but peace, was the aim of their foreign policy. This general tenor of Nazi propaganda was aimed at the Germans still more than at the outside world. Possible doubts on the part of the Germans were disposed of by ever-repeated references to the fact that most of the top men of the regime had known the horrors of the last war and that it would be sheer madness to even suspect them to wantonly drive towards a new one. We have seen how much additional support was given to Nazi propaganda with regard to the seriousness of the peace aims of Nazi foreign policy by the fact that the outside world granted this

Nazi foreign policy successes it had denied the foreign policy of the German Republic.

What had made it impossible for the Germans to back their claims for justice or even to launch timid attempts towards easing their misery and bettering their economic situation, had been the fact of unilateral disarmament. This made it easy for the Nazis to convince the Germans that in spite of rearmament, their goal was peace. It was the Germans' genuine desire for peace which induced the Nazis to pose as passionately devoted breeders of peace doves. Had things been otherwise, the Nazis would have used a different sort of propaganda! One does not get wild beasts into a fighting mood by feeding them mush and sugar pills. The Nazis made ruthless use of any and all means that promised a tightening of their grip on the Germans, and since it must be admitted that promotional psychology ranked high among their civic vices, they would certainly have stressed the bellicose implications of their aims, had there been ever so slight a chance that that type of propaganda might click with the Germans.

But if it is true that the common man in Germany did not want war, if he dreaded it, why did he start it? The answer is: He did not.

Few people of this earth are less in a position to influence the behavior and activity of their governments than were the Germans under the Nazi heel. The Nazi regime being what it was—a dictatorship of unheard-of terror—, any attempt to stop the masters of the legal mechanism who had been careful to include in their setup of straitjacketing agencies a goodly number especially designed for their own protection against the "love of the people," any such attempt would have been sheer suicide.

The day Hitler announced to a few hundred yes-men that he had given orders to start the military machine against the Poles, the precedent of Munich and the "settlement" of the Czechoslovak affair kept alive the fervent hope that this act of supreme folly would not degenerate into a general war. What could the common man do? . . . from the humblest peasant and factory worker to the richest industrialist and glittering general? What can any common man do the world over when the political leadership of his country gets the war machine started and calls upon the population to "fight for their country?" And since the Polish-German border situation, born of one of those curlicues of international law—the Versailles treaty—constituted one of the main grievances of the Germans, it was easy for Hitler and his propaganda machine to harp once again on sentiments of justice and activate thereby those driving forces which forge a functioning army out of a mass of individual citizens and which thus far the French alone have been known to resist by the unusual device of falling asleep when the charge was sounded.

Even in countries with systems of government in no way so outrageously dictatorial as the Nazis turned out to be, as in France, Great Britain, or the United States, declarations of war do not emanate from the common man but from the government, which means at best, from the representatives of the people who happen at the time to be politicians in positions of power. The only exception to this rule are the countries in which the framers of the constitution were wise enough to place the supreme decision over life and death or peace and war directly in the hands of the common man. This is the case in Switzerland where a referendum, a decision of the people, must back a declaration of war.

During the last three hundred years of the rule of "international law," politicians, including the Nazis, have declared wars when their activity or, to be more accurate, their lack of constructive activity had resulted in a situation where war, the last resort and climax of the possibilities of international law, was the only remaining method of clearing up conflicting views as to the rightfulness of an accusation or claim. When that moment comes, all statesmen, on all sides, are wont to announce to their respective peoples that this war is being fought for the sake of justice and a just cause. And whether they are right or wrong in their announcement is a matter for the victor to decide.

In the Middle Ages it was common legal practice that "if there be dispute concerning fields, vineyards, or money, . . . two be chosen to fight, and decide the cause by duel." In England, it is amusing to note, "ordeal or trial by battle" was formally stricken from the books as late as 1818. But in international relations, wars, which are mass ordeals by battle, are still practiced to determine whether God and justice are on "their" side or "ours."

But let me get back to my contention that the common man in Germany did not want war, that he dreaded it worse than hell and high water. If that is so, I hear the prosecution argue, why did the common German fight this war? Again the answer is simple. The common German fought bravely for his country, because "patriotism" is considered a virtue not only in Great Britain and the United States, but in Germany as well. The common German fought this war because he is a civilized human being whose sentiments of justice and duty compel him to do his duty. It must seem futile to look for wickedness or war-mindedness in individuals when the reasons for which modern civilized beings get involved in fighting are as obvious as that.

The common German, though he did not want nor start nor declare this war, fought bravely for the very same reasons as the common man of Great Britain or the United States.

Before the common man gets into the fight, he is mobilized, inducted, and subjected to a special military training. In submitting to these preliminary steps, he abides by the laws of his country. Draft-dodging and desertion are criminal acts not only in the United States and Great Britain but in Germany as well. Conscientious objectors are an infinitesimal portion of any civilized population. The foremost aim of military training is to make the individual realize that being a soldier is a condition which he must accept for reasons of patriotism and out of his sense of duty. Thus he is made to subordinate every personal consideration to the all-inclusive traditional aim of any war: military victory. Not only Great Britain expects every man to do his duty, and valiant soldiers and heroes who outdo what is expected of them have a claim to the admiration of their peoples and are showered with medals and iron crosses and things in all countries all over the globe. Every reason for which the boys of the United States army "did their duty" are valid for the German boys as well. And if one thinks for just one moment of the appalling sterility with which Allied statesmen stuck to the traditional ideology of war and peace and punishment in cutting up "Germany" into small rashers and collops after her so-called unconditional surrender, if one realizes how anxiously the Nazis awaited an Allied proclamation of their "war aims" in order to be able to make a desperate appeal to the Germans' instinct of self-preservation, one will no longer find it hard to understand just why the Germans fought "for their country."

There are, of course, people who are thoughtless enough to close their eyes to the whole gamut of real reasons for man's willingness to fight. They disregard, for instance, the obvious effects of military training and education and feel that they have touched the heart of the matter when they observe that the American boys fought for democracy while the German boys fought for Nazism. The truth is much, much simpler. American boys like the boys on the other side of the lines, fought "for their country" which is a general term designed to cover all that is connected with a man's abiding by the laws of his country: donning the uniform, undergoing military training, liking or disliking the strange experience of being crowded together with a herd of other males, being educated for death, and getting ready to die joyfully for "the greater glory of his country."

A Last Word to the Jury

A Last Word to the Jury

This was my plea.

If it were part of a real jury trial in which some individual had been brought to court to answer a well drawn-up indictment, I could now, on the strength of what I have said, await the verdict of the jury in confidence.

But the situation has little to do with a real trial. In so far as the German people are concerned, it has been a very lopsided affair. The verdict of "guilty" was anticipated and in place of the customary charge to the jury, the judges went ahead meting out punishment over the heads of the jurors.

This is what is called grand strategy and world politics. The present plight of the Germans is the result, and a tragic one indeed, especially when viewed as but one, albeit essential, element in the whole dismal and discouraging picture of the whole world today. The punishment of the German people which began with the demand for unconditional surrender and which was further mapped out at Yalta, Teheran, and Potsdam with supreme disregard for the fate of man, was conceived—the whole idle talk about democracy notwithstanding—by judges who went in wholeheartedly for what politicians in similar positions—and in this group Hitler and his kind are well in their place—have been going in for over the centuries, the favorite pastime of so-called great men: the management of international affairs according to the concepts of so-called international law which actually has as much to do with what you and I mean by "law" as fire has to do with water and is in truth but a primitive farce of it, a caricature and replica of the law of the jungle.

As far as the common mortal is concerned, he suffers from it all and is graciously allowed to foot the bill. As far as the "great men" are concerned, they exhaust themselves in totally futile attempts to bring about peaceful coexistence of the peoples of this earth as they continue to try to make sense out of the application of the senseless concepts now prevailing in international politics. It was said after the first World War, and it has been proved during the various economic crises that followed, that exacting reparations from the population of a vanquished, materially exhausted, and economically shattered country, is sheer lunacy. Yet, right after this last war, the repetition of such economic lunacy is one of the principal preoccupations of the great men of the victorious nations. These great men are all set to go on leading stricken humanity around the vicious circle of war and peace, peace and war. And after they have gone through their act, they die or commit suicide or are hanged or retire and work on their memoirs, those extraordinary documents of self-justification and self-glorification in which the great men let gaping humanity in on the details of the futility of their efforts.

However, we have shown no particular interest in great men in this plea. We have been concerned with the fate of millions and millions of little men. And however great or small the leading great men are or have been, however rashly they may have acted in anticipating the verdict of the jury, nothing irreparable has been done. The last word still rests with the jury.

Are the Germans "just getting what they have coming to them?" The consequences of this war represent punishment for them on a scale which exceeds human imagination. Look at their cities, their homes and places of work in ruins! Imagine the sorrow and misery which the death of millions and millions of sons, brothers, husbands, and fathers has brought to the present generation. Think of the plight of the German women shouldering the gigantic task of rebuilding and reconstruction. Think of all that, and it will dawn on you that no human mind could possibly devise a more thorough punishment—and one may well ask whether this is not enough.

On the other hand, if I or any other thinking person had been given the task of working out a plan designed to keep the evil spirit of the Nazis alive in the German people, to kindle in them a desire for revenge, to lay the foundation for their eventually becoming ready to listen to another Hitler, to nullify the horror which gripped the German population when confronted with a true picture of Nazi crimes, then no better plan could be invented than the treatment now being dished out to the Germans, not according to plan but according to a lack of plan, a hodge-podge of "policy" based on "international law" and the bickerings of the victors among themselves.

As far as the Germans are concerned, they will readily respond to any positive move made by the only people in a position to make such a move, the Americans, the jury I am addressing. There is no people on this earth more willing to renounce the mere thought of future wars than the Germans, so gruesomely stricken by destiny. There is no people on this earth more ready to foil any future attempt at rape by Black, Brown, or Red Fascists than the Germans, so utterly betrayed and misled by a gang of public-welfare hucksters who tried to pass off brutality as manliness, high-sounding phraseology as serious concern with the common good and who drove my people to the edge of the abyss under fake promises of a golden future. There is no people on this earth more eager to help, as free men, in the rebuilding of Europe than the Germans who, as Hitler-ridden slaves, were misled into plunging the Continent into misery.

But can you be expected to kiss and make up and let bygones be bygones? Why not? Because it has never been done before? Because it would mean applying to international affairs a pattern of behavior which is one of the most potent factors toward workable human relations? Because it would conform to the most sublime tenets of our Christian heritage? Because it would mean a clean break with the past, a past from which the entire world is suffering right now? Because it would mean an attempt to draw the only sensible conclusion of wars, of blood, sweat, and tears in humanity's experience under the reign of "international law?" Because it might mean that battered and suffering humanity all over the world would finally see some hope for a better future, that uneasiness would yield its place to hopefulness? Because it might mean that the bickerings of your conscience, prompted by the use of the atomic bomb, could be soothed by the hope that it might never have to be used again for destructive purposes?

There are a thousand reasons why "kiss and make up" is the only thing to do to give humanity and the Germans a break through intelligent management of international relations. There are a thousand and one reasons why this is the only way to replace declarations as empty as they are bombastic on "peace and justice for all" or "a new era in world politics" by true service to peaceful coexistence of the various nations of this earth.

What can you, the jury I have addressed in pleading the case of the Germans, do about it?

It would not be fair if this writer—after exposing in his plea for the Germans how surprisingly little the common man in Germany could do once he was faced with that ruthless gang of Nazi gangsters —were now to proceed devising programs and drawing up declarations as to what the "United States" should do and should not do with regard to "Germany." It would mean that I dared to place on your shoulders a responsibility which is not yours. You do not make the foreign policy of your country—not more so than the Germans did in their country.

Any outline of what might be a desirable foreign policy would be a waste of time. As things are, those who make the foreign policy of a country do not allow the tenor and course of their activities to be determined or even influenced by the thought and argument of an outsider. The actions and reactions of political activists and other office-holders have always been and still are almost completely divorced from the efforts of the human mind to work out solutions of the great problems of the time and formulate their conclusions on paper.

Politicians do not act in a certain way because they were impressed by a book they happened to read; they act for the most part because they are in a position where "something has got to be done." And in doing something they lean heavily on the advice of diplomats and experts who are, to the great detriment of humanity, completely sold to the traditional way of approaching problems of world politics by way of the murderous tenets of "international law." And once the course of their action is set and implemented by the usual military, legislative, and diplomatic trimmings, once the verdict of the jury is anticipated, they try to talk you into agreeing with them and eventually take your lack of interest, your apathy, or your honest "don't know" for acquiescence and consent.

What you can do about it is to give some thought to the situation of the Germans and perhaps form your own equitable opinion on the subject of this key problem of the present turmoil. And then you can go on and give some thought to the still more fundamental question as to why the fate of the world is still, is again being handled according to the bloody pattern of a century-old tradition of perfect failures. You are fortunate to be able to think about it all and to voice your opinion without being faced with threats from a medieval Gestapo, with concentration camps, with public disgrace to yourself and your family, or with whatever coercive measures the former and present dictatorial regimes have used and are using to keep their peoples in bondage and slavery.

The Author's Credentials

The Author's Credentials

I have pleaded the German cause, and some members of the jury will want to see my credentials.

I am a naturalized American and was born in 1910 in Magdeburg, Germany. I was brought up in a typical German-Prussian family with my brother and sister. My earliest recollections go back to the last years of the first World War and to the noisy wooden-soled shoes we wore because there just was no leather for the average purse at that time. I went to the *Realgymnasium* and was sufficiently undernourished to be selected for the *Quäker-Speisung*—a distribution of crullers and hot chocolate arranged twice a week by those legendary Christians who live up to the faith they profess. I remember the amazing German runaway inflation mainly because of the grave and worried expression on my parents' faces. They were not smart enough to gamble on the stock market and watched their savings, invested in government bonds, go up in smoke and general misery. I recall the wonderful steadfastness with which my parents, city people, faced the seemingly impossible task of seeing three fast-growing children through, by raising their own food in a little "victory" garden. I got as good an education as my parents, with a sublime display of self-abnegation and nearly complete renunciation of every small luxury like smoking or an occasional concert or play, could afford to give me. I was lucky enough to be initiated into the world of music by learning to play an instrument and joining some of the numerous private quartets and orchestras. I joined actively and with enthusiasm the world of sports. I remember graduation day, a family feast of joy if there ever was one.

Politics? Oh, yes, politics—that was a very unimportant matter in our lives. To be sure, there had been great changes; there had even been a revolution of very unpleasant memory, with shootings in the streets and general disorder. Now people were said to be governing themselves; but, absorbed as they were in relentless and full-time efforts to meet the basic needs and live as decently and as inconspicuously as nice people do, imbued with the idea that all these tricky things should be taken

care of by people who knew what they were doing and were equipped for it, politics ran a very
poor last among the preoccupations of our family.
True enough, measured by the number of political
parties fighting each other and fighting for votes,
there seemed to be surprisingly many experts or
would-be experts around. There even were growing numbers of people who preferred rabble-rousing politics to the difficulties of making an honest,
decent living. But that was their business. True,
one donned one's Sunday clothes on Election Day
and went to the polls because it was said to be so
very important. But otherwise concern with politics did not go too far beyond reading the newspaper to which one subscribed.

I had chosen the profession of lawyer as the one
best suited to my human and professional aspira-
tions. Like the large majority of boys and girls
whose parents had to perform miracles of budget-
ing to pay for university fees and living expenses in
a university town, my student days had nothing
to do with the gay life of student-prince fame; it
was hard work and study, and again there was no
time for and little interest in politics. There were,
to be sure, some noisy groups of youngsters who
professed interest in politics and who occasionally
made a nuisance of themselves by disturbing the
quiet of university life, but, being numerically

negligible, the rest of us paid little attention to them.

The end of my studies coincided with the victory of the Nazis. This seemingly innocent victory by a determined group of reckless political activists was to prove of far greater consequence than anyone seemed ready or prepared to realize.

For me, the nature of the amazing phenomenon made itself felt in various ways. Having pursued special studies in criminal law, I published an article in one of the innumerable German law reviews. It was noticed by one of those Nazi scribes who had already ensconced themselves as arbiters and masters of the publishing trade. Nevertheless, I proceeded to enlarge it into a more comprehensive study on various aspects of the political sciences. But every publisher I approached began by asking the fatal question: How does your book deal with the Nazis and National Socialism? And after I had given the answer, no one dared to publish it. They all had had a hard time building up their firms and keeping them going, and a few experiences had quickly shown them that the Nazis in power meant business, that they were ready and quite able to ruin anyone who didn't fall in line.—

I did not take it too much to heart. For me, this business of writing and thinking about social affairs was just an avocation anyway, and I thought

I might get along for a while without publishing my masterpiece. The storm would blow over soon and things in my country would be as they had always been and as they should be. Meanwhile, I would work at my doctor's thesis and prepare more seriously than ever for my chosen profession. Nazis or no Nazis, life was going on. The efforts of my parents were about to bear fruit. One of their boys was about to join one of the most respected professions, that of law, and they could look forward to seeing him get established in an office and have his name on the door for all to know and to show that a member of the family had made good. Life was going on.

By 1935 the Nazis in power had made quite a bit of progress in their methodical nazification of German life; it had become practically impossible to become a lawyer without joining up with the Nazis in one way or another. The changes decreed by the Nazis had most thoroughly affected my chosen profession. Law had become a tool in the hands of fiends, even though one hoped against hope that this could not go on much longer. The lawyer had been ruled out of his age-old role of friend and helper of the individual in need.

But, after all, I was a German; this was my own country; my pedigree could pass muster under the sternest rules of Nazi biology; I was a pure Aryan;

I had had no part in leftist politics. It was so easy . . . Just a little kick to your conscience if it could possibly bother you because you were one of the few who had had an early glimpse at what Nazi politics and Nazi government really meant, or . . . just join up . . . Try to make the best of it . . . and sun yourself in the official verbiage of patriotism, community feelings, the apparent success of the Nazi New Deal, and what not . . .

But I couldn't. I just couldn't.

Now what? I couldn't go on living on my parents' resources. Wherever I looked, the problem was everywhere the same. I could not publish anything unless I embraced Nazism. I could not even earn a living by working with my hands unless I embraced Nazism. And then, too, there was the family; there were my father and mother who had lived and worked all their lives with only one thought in mind: to get the children well started in life, and who were now waiting for the years of old age to rejoice in their children's success and to reap the fruit of their labor and struggle.

It was not easy to break it all up. What could I do? I was not brought up to commit murder nor educated or prepared for political underground plotting. Leave the country; it seemed the only solution.—Father and mother had to be told. Oh, they took it bravely. But there remained with me the vivid memory of the sorrow on their faces when in early 1936 I told them of my decision to turn my back on our Nazi-ridden land.

Two close friends, faced with much the same problem, chose to stay on. We did not know at the time which course would be the more difficult: to go on facing it in our own country or to try to make a go of it in foreign lands. Both my friends came through. Most of them did—my parents completely bombed out, destitute and sharing the vicious fate to which old people under Russian occupation are destined: slow starvation; their relatives driven from the East and scattered all over Germany; sister Waldtraut perished in Russia; brother Günther engrossed in the full-time task of keeping his little family with two children going. Friend Hans seemed to have made it all right, but I have had no news from him since his infant son died for want of food and adequate medical care. Friend Willi, after having been dragged over the years from high positions in the German automobile industry through prisons, before People's Courts, to concentration camp and punitive company for not having made common cause with the Nazis and for having spoken his mind, is now patiently trying to rebuild a little factory from the remnants of a huge war plant which was blown to bits.

From the moment I arrived in France—practically the only European country still offering a fairly liberal asylum to foreigners—my life was of course permanently clouded by the *Unheil* I felt brewing "over there." Pleasant experiences with the common run of Frenchmen ran parallel to unpleasant experiences with the crowd of early refugees from Nazism who had established themselves within the atmosphere of hospitality which France, as so often before in her history, had extended to these unfortunate exiles. Faced with a late-comer, the majority of them—both the Jews and the mixed crowd of leftist runaways—behaved the way any group of humans more or less comfortably settled in a railroad compartment will behave when a new arrival tries to claim a seat. It did not matter too much. Since there was practically no one among these great men with their futures behind them who succeeded in placing serious concern with general problems above his own individual mishap, their refusal to move over made little difference.

The help of Swedish friends took care of most of my animal needs and made it possible for me to devote considerable time to further study of German and international problems. With a few reflections I even managed to break into print, but of course, at a time of general effervescence created by a blunt, happy-unhappy revival of brazen European power politics, the voices of reason were mere whisperings in the tumult of a mad carnival.

The general tenor of this pre-war European carnival of the late 30s did not lack a certain bitter flavor for me. After I had left my country because I did not want to play ball with the Nazis, I had to watch the mad spectacle of respected and respectable governments all over Europe turning veritable somersaults in their effort to gain the Nazis' approval as efficient caddies. My only consolation was the fact that the Nazi crowd had deemed me an opponent worthy of being deprived of his German nationality.

Then war broke out. If nothing else could bring the end of Nazidom, for the sake of the world and the Germans, this war would. And that was a ray of hope in this night of horror which every thinking person felt at the prospect of another carnage ravaging the unfortunate inhabitants of the Continent. The war got off to a slow start. Nothing happened in the West except that the intricacies of French precautions against enemy aliens struck with full fury the only "enemies" they could readily lay hands on—the refugees.

To be sure, you could prove that you had nothing to do with Nazi Germany, that you would not move one finger to help the Nazis get away with

173

murder on a large scale; but *you* try to explain something like that to a squad of heavily armed French warriors under orders to arrest you. *You* try to explain something like that to a crowd watching you being marched under heavy guard to a concentration camp, a crowd screaming at you, throwing stones at you, spitting at you—or better: don't try, it might make matters worse.

Then came months of concentration camp behind barbed wires, under repeated pressure (applied by this or that officer interested in a bit of head money) to escape the present unpleasantness by signing up for the Foreign Legion, that charming melting-pot of the toughies of the world at the end of their rope.

Well, somehow it seemed natural that the French should do everything possible to avoid unpleasant surprises from a group of foreigners living in their country; and so you garbed yourself in hope, a hope based on the certainty that at the end of it all there would be a world, including your German countrymen, freed from the Nazi yoke.

After several months came our "liberation." It meant the promotion from the rank of a concentration camp inmate to membership in a workers' battalion, now allowed, though still under heavy guard and of course without arms, to carry a pick-axe, a shovel, or whatever tool was needed to accomplish our contribution to the humane cause of a variety of pioneering tasks.

When finally the phony war degenerated into the real shooting match, we were transferred to the North. This was going to be the real thing. Maybe we would get close enough to action to get what it takes to free a man from any curse and evil fate. It had become so burdensome to carry the cross of "being a German" in addition to the pick-axe that we often wished for it. But the powers that be must have decided otherwise.

Upon our arrival at Le Mans we learned that another scheme had been cooked up to put our shoveling capacities to better use: the British Expeditionary Forces were about to entrench themselves solidly in Brittany. An arrangement on some higher level of command had provided for the *prestataires* (the technical name for us concentration camp promotees) to be lend-leased to the B.E.F. Anyone without a hernia was welcome. Actually what it all amounted to was a change of attire. Whereas with the French we wore a fantastic mixture of civilian knickerbockers and old left-over-from-the-first-World-War light blue field jackets, the Britishers stuck us into amazing outfits of beige corduroy with a dark blue beret. And then they gave us a sailor's bag to carry our belongings in.

After a few days of initiation into the mysteries of the British manual of arms, we were transported to our camp in the center of Brittany. Some officers, seasoned experts in the art of ordering around colonials and other second-rate humans, were our masters and a couple of Tommies our foremen. You were of course at a certain advantage if you could say a few words in their language. The yearning of a boozy Tommy for company was sufficient to establish a pipe-line to the officers' splendid supply of whisky and gin or to the troops' depot of French wines and exotic rum—which made for occasional pleasant moments of alcoholic oblivion and brotherhood.

After the usual morning parade during which each face was closely scrutinized for a clean fresh shave—a rather time-consuming necessity if you consider that we were a gang of some three hundred slaves—we were marched off to our posts, the masters of our fate apparently taking a certain pride in how nicely those sons . . . had learned to swing their arms the British way. And then, all day long, we made French peasants unhappy by cutting down their most beautiful trees, leveling their grounds with supreme disregard for growing crops, and laying rails.

Our transfer to British military rule had brought

176

all mail service to a standstill; newspapers were also banned, and it was merely by accident that we learned of Italy's having performed what President Roosevelt chose publicly to refer to as one of her historic "stabs in the back." The general absence of news did make for considerable nervousness. That most of us felt pretty certain that if we were caught by the Germans, there would not be much to look forward to, was not exactly apt to ease the strain. Then one afternoon we were called to form in ranks and received the news that the evacuation of the B.E.F. was under consideration, but that, under any circumstances, we would be evacuated with the British. The next morning, when we awoke, the Britishers had left. And then a mad race began to reach the coast.

I narrowly escaped being shot by a French gendarme who wouldn't understand that we just had to get away. That we did get away—in the course of a nerve-racking and yet elating escape—was principally due to the combined efforts of French army and navy officers at Lorient. An exciting trip in nutshells over choppy seas, transshipment to a French warship off Bordeaux, arrival at Casablanca. Military prison, internment barracks, endless questioning, then weeks and weeks of internment again until everyone was so fed up with those foreigners that we got discharge papers, followed by life on a pig-breeding farm with Arabs and mules and dogs.

Apparently quiet months. But in spite of everything, you were still very much a part of the general turmoil; you felt like getting back into it, somehow, some way. Where could you turn? In which direction could you try, should you try, if not in the direction of legendary America? Close contact with Frenchmen over the years had made me believe as in a basic truth that eventually the United States would come in and finish the whole business. Threads were spun, good friends in the U.S. helped, and the day of embarkment on one of the refugee ships arrived. This was toward the end of November, 1941. No one doubted that the U.S. would, at long last, come into the war, but it was the general opinion that nothing of the sort could be expected before late 1942. Thanks to the Japanese attack on Pearl Harbor it happened sooner. I was still on the ocean. Good luck and bad luck at the same time. Good luck because now the end of the war had really moved into sight; bad luck because the past two years had made the idea of again being slated for refugee treatment a haunting obsession.

And then the unbelievable happened.

It was not the Statue of Liberty which turned me inside out, it was nothing but the way we were received. It was nothing but the way the American immigration officials checked our papers, looked at us and asked a few questions, not without openly sharing in our joy at having finally reached a safe harbor. The miracle was simply that we were being treated like human beings.

And then you could leave the ship and go wherever you were expected. Of course you didn't quite dare to believe in miracles, and so you waited a while, looking over your shoulder, as it were, fully expecting to be caught in another of those refugee schemes. But no, they really let you alone.

Of course you soon had new worries to cope with. You can live on your friends' hospitality for just so long. After that you had better look for work. But in that too this strange country had a surprise in store for you. Over there they wanted you to be a Nazi before they would allow you to work; and in France you needed an official worker's permit which you couldn't get; but here, you could just work for what anyone thought you were worth.

Being hard pressed and without so much as a penny to my name, I started the way I thought best for putting something by against another rainy day. *Arbeit schändet nicht*—I couldn't help thinking of one of the sayings I had practically grown up on: honest work is nothing to be ashamed of. And so, cheerfully, I slipped into one of those occupations so many newcomers began with: for a while I took a job as a butler.

Once during that time I was invited (not in my capacity of butler) to address a gathering of lawyers on Nazi law and all its implications. Then, when the war machine was running in high gear and people in command of various foreign languages were sought after, I joined the march of history in one of the agencies of the government (not the O.W.I.) primarily concerned with certain special aspects of the war effort.

That is my story.

If I have the courage to present a plea for the Germans, if I am willing to face whatever consequences such a step may entail, it is largely due to the experiences I have had since my arrival in these United States; it is due to the most revealing contacts I have had with what I took to be typical Americans, honest, decent, and hard-working people who like others to be frank because they are frank themselves; who let people have their say because they like to have their say too when they feel like it; who are as remote from malice and as allergic to injustice as any people I have known—and in whose hands, as little or as much as they asked for it or wanted it, the fate of Western civilization, with all its achievements and imperfections, rests.